School-based Teacher Training

a handbook for tutors and mentors

Education at SAGE

SAGE is a leading international publisher of journals, books, and electronic media for academic, educational, and professional markets.

Our education publishing includes:

- accessible and comprehensive texts for aspiring education professionals and practitioners looking to further their careers through continuing professional development

- inspirational advice and guidance for the classroom

- authoritative state of the art reference from the leading authors in the field

Find out more at: **www.sagepub.co.uk/education**

School-based Teacher Training

a handbook for tutors and mentors

Edited by

Elizabeth White and Joy Jarvis

Los Angeles | London | New Delhi
Singapore | Washington DC

Los Angeles | London | New Delhi
Singapore | Washington DC

SAGE Publications Ltd
1 Oliver's Yard
55 City Road
London EC1Y 1SP

SAGE Publications Inc.
2455 Teller Road
Thousand Oaks, California 91320

SAGE Publications India Pvt Ltd
B 1/I 1 Mohan Cooperative Industrial Area
Mathura Road
New Delhi 110 044

SAGE Publications Asia-Pacific Pte Ltd
3 Church Street
#10-04 Samsung Hub
Singapore 049483

First published 2013

Library of Congress Control Number: 2012938830

British Library Cataloguing in Publication data

A catalogue record for this book is available from
the British Library

Editor: Jude Bowen
Assistant editor: Miriam Davey
Assistant production editor: Nicola Marshall
Production manager: Bill Antrobus
Copyeditor: H A Fairlie
Proofreader: Caroline Stock
Marketing manager: Lorna Patkai
Cover design: Wendy Scott
Typeset by Kestrel Data, Exeter, Devon
Printed by: CPI Group (UK) Ltd,
Croydon, CR0 4YY

ISBN 978-1-4462-5464-6
ISBN 978-1-4462-5465-3 (pbk)

Contents

List of figures

List of tables

Foreword

It is a time of great change in teaching and teacher education, with a shift toward school-led teacher training and the introduction of Teaching Schools. Schools will take on increasing responsibility for the professional development of trainee and newly qualified teachers in their workplace. The editors of this book are passionate about the quality of initial teacher education; they believe that new teachers must have the opportunity to establish their professional values, identity, knowledge and practice in order to provide an excellent learning experience for all pupils.

The initial teacher education partnership between schools and universities is in a state of flux. As new roles develop and the responsibilities of the various players are realigned, it is vital that the wealth of practice experience, the criticality and rigour of academic study and the opportunity to have a vision for education which exceeds the immediate context are preserved. This presents a challenge for us all. It is a challenge we must rise to in order to ensure that professionally committed teachers in our schools are able to offer the best possible learning experiences for all pupils.

This book will be a useful resource for anyone working with trainee and newly qualified teachers. It offers a way for teachers to manage their own professional development when taking on the changing and challenging responsibilities of a school-based 'teacher educator'.

Dr Mary Read
Dean of School of Education, University of Hertfordshire

Acknowledgements

This book has been written to help teachers who are taking on the role of teacher educators. We would like to thank all the trainees, teachers and teacher educators who have contributed to our research directly and those who have influenced us while we have been working collaboratively on initial and continuing professional development programmes at the University of Hertfordshire.

Our thanks go to Jude Bowen and Miriam Davey at Sage for their guidance in the production of this book.

Preface

Outstanding learning in schools depends on the quality of the teachers. Initial teacher training enables individuals to be effective, purposeful practitioners and reflective professionals able to creatively prepare future generations for the challenges ahead. Taking on the new role of teacher educator as a tutor or mentor of early career teachers is a challenging task for experienced teachers in any setting. In interviews we found that teachers with this additional responsibility initially assumed that they only needed experience as a teacher to train others effectively. However, this view changed in their first year working in schools to support trainee teachers as they realised that additional practices and knowledge of teacher education are required to meet the needs of their trainees. It can be difficult for teachers who do this work based in a school to access the expertise of other teacher educators in order to develop their practice. It is for these teachers in particular that this book is written. We hope you will find this a practical resource to guide your professional development and to enable you to be confident and secure in your practice.

Each of the authors has drawn on their experience, their own research and wider research from the field of teacher education to underpin their contribution.

Structure of the book

The book is in two parts. Part A is focused on how teacher educators develop their own professional knowledge and understanding. Part B is designed to enable you to analyse many aspects of your practice so that you can dip in to the chapters that are the most appropriate for your current responsibilities. The role of the teacher educator is underpinned by scholarship (engaging with educational theory and research and integrating it with practice) and research (contributing to original research in the field of education). Our desire is that teacher educators will aspire to developing high level skills and confidence in practitioner research so that they can support their trainees in enquiry and action research activities. We see Chapters 9 and 10 as the pinnacle of the book for this reason.

Throughout Part B resources are provided to nurture the development of the trainee towards reaching and going beyond the specific professional standards applicable in your context.

Further support

As we have edited this book we have realised there is so much more that we would like to share with you. We would be very interested in your feedback about what you have found helpful and what else you would find useful for your on-going development as a school-based teacher educator. Within the School of Education at the University of Hertfordshire we have a wide range of expertise and welcome working in partnership with schools – this could include consultancy, research projects, professional learning conversations, running bespoke courses or exploring on-going partnership working.

Elizabeth White and Joy Jarvis
e.j.white@herts.ac.uk   j.jarvis@herts.ac.uk
School of Education, University of Hertfordshire

About the editors and contributors

The editors

Joy Jarvis worked in primary schools and as an advisory teacher for deaf children before coming to the University of Hertfordshire to lead a course in deaf education. She has developed approaches for supporting new teacher educators in the School of Education. In her role as Associate Dean, she is currently researching student-staff partnership in learning and teaching.

Elizabeth White has been working with the GTP for five years while being employed as a secondary science teacher. She is currently the Deputy Programme Director for the Hertfordshire Regional Partnership GTP. The GTP is one of the employment-based routes into teaching where it is possible to train and qualify as a teacher while working in a school. Her research has included a self study of her experience as a new teacher educator developing a new aspect to her identity and she is currently researching how to support new subject tutors in developing the subject knowledge of trainee teachers.

The contributors

Lynn Chapman is the Programme Director of the PGCE secondary programme, and science PGCE course tutor at the University of Hertfordshire. Lynn's current research focuses on apprenticeship learning using real world experiences through the medium of Forum Theatre to develop a greater quality and depth of reflection. Prior to taking up her role at Hertfordshire, she was a science teacher in a number of schools and was head of department. Lynn has published previously as co-editor of the Key Stage 3 scheme of work, *Connecting Science* (Hodder Education). She also has a chapter, 'Physics for 4-Year-Olds: Promoting Open and Focused Exploration for Young Children in Everyday Contexts' in *Science Education at the Nexus of Theory and Practice*, edited by Y. J. Lee and A. L. Tan (2008, Sense).

Bushra Connors is a Senior Lecturer in the School of Education at the University of Hertfordshire. She is currently teaching on the Doctorate in Education programme. Bushra developed her ideas on science teaching during her twenty years' experience as a physicist, a science teacher and head of department. Her previous publications have been concerned with behaviour management in schools and recent conference papers have been about the use of narrative methods in assessing students and the use of metaphor in pedagogy. Together with Lynn Chapman, she has been collaborating in an action research project with science trainee teachers involving the emancipatory use of theatrical techniques, drawing upon the work of Augusto Boal, to assist trainees to share their collective experiences of the journey from novice to experienced teacher.

Lara Fuller is the current Programme Director for Education CPD at the University at Hertfordshire. Previously, she worked as a primary school teacher and as a local authority adviser working with schools to develop their practice and understanding of assessment for learning. She now works closely with schools to help them to develop their CPD programmes and this learning community has become the focus for her research.

Sally Graham is a leading teacher educator with particular expertise in coaching and mentoring, professional learning and leadership. After a career in primary schools leading to deputy headship, she now has the role of director of the University of Hertfordshire's Centre for Coaching and Mentoring. In this role Sally leads national conferences, short courses and bespoke consultancy for business organisations, voluntary sector groups and educational providers as well as the managing of specialist postgraduate courses and qualifications. Sally's research interests include relational coaching, action research and arts-informed inquiry.

Phil Lenten taught in secondary schools in Hertfordshire for over 20 years, where he also had long-term responsibility for professional development. This experience as a teacher educator led to an opportunity to establish and run a new PGCE course at Middlesex University before moving to employment-based ITT at the University of Hertfordshire. Over 10 years he has played a lead role in developing the Graduate Teacher Programme into one of the largest employment-based programmes of its kind in the country, acknowledged by Ofsted as a grade 1 provider. Phil also manages a successful programme for Overseas Trained Teachers. His particular interest is in developing Masters level work as an integral element of GTP. Phil is an experienced external examiner for GTP and OTTP.

Amanda Roberts worked in schools in Hertfordshire for 20 years, culminating in a headship, prior to joining the University of Hertfordshire. She moved on to run an educational consultancy company, providing support for learning in a variety of contexts including schools in challenging circumstances. Amanda is currently Programme Director for the MSc in Practice-Based Research. Her previous publications have focused on school improvement, with a recent emphasis on student leadership. Her current research focuses on the development of students and staff as academic writers.

Mike Stevens has worked for over 30 years in Hertfordshire secondary schools, with over 15 years as a deputy headteacher and most recently as a headteacher. For several years he chaired the Stevenage CPD group, which collaboratively introduced performance management to all Stevenage secondary schools and has worked closely as a teacher educator in the role of professional mentor with the University of Hertfordshire both with PGCE and GTP trainees. In recent years, he has taught in Professional Studies on the PGCE programme and is a Visiting Tutor on the Graduate Teacher Programme at the University of Hertfordshire. He is currently working with the Stevenage Educational Trust in exploring the cross-phase delivery of CPD.

Hilary Taylor is a Senior Lecturer at the University of Hertfordshire, with an interest in the professional development of teachers at all stages of their career. She is Programme Director for the Masters in Teaching and Learning and is a lead tutor for the CPD Masters programme. She works closely with schools to develop a research and enquiry-based approach to professional development and school improvement. Hilary's research has included case studies of teachers engaging in research activity both in the UK and overseas. She is currently researching the nature of teachers' professional knowledge in different contexts and exploring professional identity as they progress in their careers.

Abbreviations

CPD   Continuing Professional Development

GTP   Graduate Teacher Programme

ICT   Information and Communications Technology

ITT   Initial Teacher Training

NQT   Newly Qualified Teacher

OTTP   Overseas Trained Teacher Programme

PGCE   Postgraduate Certificate in Education

SKfT   Subject Knowledge for Teaching

PART A

HOW TEACHER EDUCATORS DEVELOP THEIR OWN PROFESSIONAL KNOWLEDGE AND UNDERSTANDING

1

The professional development of teacher educators

Elizabeth White and Joy Jarvis

This chapter covers:

- who teacher educators are and what they do;
- what we know about the early stages of professional development of teacher educators;
- how you can use this book to chart a pathway for your personal and professional development as a teacher educator.

What is a teacher educator and who takes on this role?

Teacher educators facilitate the professional development of teachers by providing learning opportunities for teachers through a variety of means and in a range of contexts. The teachers may be at any stage of their teaching career; however, within this book we are focusing on nurturing trainee teachers and newly qualified teachers in particular. Teacher educators can be involved in the preparation, leading, facilitation and evaluation of a multiplicity of activities, some of which might include:

- leading sessions on pre-service training programmes;

- carrying out observations and giving feedback;

- encouraging teachers to reflect on and evaluate their own teaching;

- providing on-going support as and when needed;

- facilitating training opportunities such as observations and team teaching;

- leading professional development sessions;

- providing resources and guidance;

- research into aspects of education.

Many initial teacher education programmes are situated in higher education institutions with university-based teacher educators. Experienced teachers in schools also work as teacher educators, supporting the learning of trainee teachers and newly qualified teachers in the classroom by taking on roles as mentors or tutors in partnership with providers of initial teacher education. In addition, the growth of school-led initial teacher training routes means that there are teachers who take on extended teacher education roles while working within schools. Additionally, subject specialists and advanced skills teachers who are helping trainees and new teachers develop their teaching skills have a role as teacher educators. Leaders of professional development in school and in further education colleges who have responsibility for the initial and continuing professional development of teachers may have this role alongside an organisational overview. In summary, there is a diverse group of individuals who we would view as having this privileged role of being teacher educators.

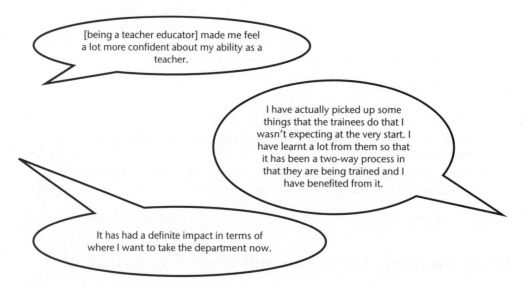

Figure 1.1 The voice of new teacher educators

Although there are clearly benefits from undertaking this role (see Figure 1.1), it can be extremely challenging and teacher educators need to look after themselves first in order to take better care of others later. This is why Part A is focused on you as a teacher educator and the community in which you work, rather than on your practice. It is helpful initially to reflect on what we know about the development of teacher educators.

The early stages of professional development of teacher educators

Teacher educators who are teaching about teaching are often referred to as second order practitioners in the literature about their professional development. This term was originally used by Murray and Male (2005) to distinguish the work of teacher educators from that of first order practitioners, i.e. teachers, who are working in the original field. These terms help us to appreciate the layered nature of the teacher educator's role. Teacher educators are increasingly undertaking the dual role of teacher and teacher educator. In this case these professionals are working both as first and second order practitioners. Whether you are working as a second order practitioner for a little, some or most of your time, and whether this is in one or several workplaces, much of the research about the early stages of professional development of teacher educators will have some useful messages even though most of these teacher educators were in higher education institutions.

Becoming a second order practitioner does not happen automatically and may involve a period of de-skilling while moving from expert in one field to novice in another (Berry and Loughran, 2002; Harrison and McKeon, 2008; Clemans et al., 2010; White, 2011). This research indicates that new teacher educators initially rely on classroom experience. After a time they realise that first order practice is not sufficient and additional knowledge and practices of teacher education are needed. This occurs with a growing understanding of the needs of their learners and through involvement with the professional community of teacher educators.

The process of becoming a teacher educator may initially involve identifying transferable skills and strategies from teaching; bringing your credibility as a first order practitioner and reconstructing your pedagogy to meet the learning needs of your trainees (Boyd and Harris, 2010). The literature reports that initially teacher educators appreciate the need to model good practice but do not appreciate the need to be explicit about modelling. The importance of making hidden professional knowledge explicit to trainee teachers is explored in Chapter 4.

There are many examples in the literature of new teacher educators in higher education institutions learning from formal and informal practices in their workplace, e.g. McKeon and Harrison (2010), and of early professional learning being facilitated by participation in a community of teacher educators. When new teacher educators work alongside experienced teacher educators they move towards full participation in the community of practice and gain confidence and expertise. Lave and Wenger (1991) propose that professional identity is formed in a community of practice. Swennen et al. (2008) also suggest that the professional identity of teacher educators is built through socialisation within this community. This means that the new teacher educators who are involved in their own workplace, remote from a wider community of teacher educators, may find it difficult to develop this identity, and may not even see themselves as teacher educators, since this is one role among many that they have in their workplace. Chapter 3 looks at ways of developing a new identity as a teacher educator and you may need to look for opportunities for becoming part of a community of teacher educators locally or online.

Another theme in the literature regarding the professional development of teacher educators is their need to have an over-riding enquiry perspective on their work (Cochran-Smith, 2003) rather than seeing enquiry as a separate activity among many. This means that teacher educators educate themselves and each other by regarding the work of others as developmental and open to interrogation. New teacher educators do not need rigid induction programmes for their early development but creative ways to explore and work together with prospective teachers and experienced teachers in communities of learners. Teacher educators develop through integrating research and practice (Murray and Male, 2005). This is explored further in Chapters 9 and 10.

Charting a pathway for your personal and professional development as a teacher educator

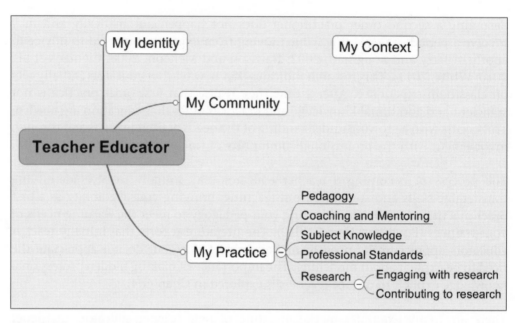

Figure 1.2   Aspects of the professional development of teacher educators

The background of Figure 1.2 represents the **context** within which you are working. As a teacher your immediate context is your whole school setting. Chapter 2 looks at you as a teacher educator within this setting to help you identify how your role fits into the wider picture.

As you take on the role of teacher educator and start to develop your **identity** as a second order practitioner, you will need to consider the changing aspects of your role. Chapter 3 will focus on helping to develop your identity as a teacher educator and suggests you integrate into a **community** or develop your own community with practitioners undertaking similar responsibilities. When you have looked at this chapter for your own personal development you will also find it useful to consider how you will nurture your trainees as they develop their identity as teachers and find appropriate communities in which they can share their professional learning with others. It may even be that you are responsible for ensuring that there is an enquiring community in which your trainees can learn together with other staff.

As a first order practitioner you will already have a wealth of knowledge and skills for your professional **practice**. This is now the foundational knowledge that you will be bringing to your new role as a second order practitioner. In Part B of the book we will explore how you can enhance and extend your knowledge and skills.

In Chapter 4 you will be invited to examine your own beliefs about learning and teaching as a basis for your work in enabling trainees to recognise how their beliefs impact on their teaching. You will be able to identify key aspects of your first order practice that you will be explicitly modelling, i.e. demonstrating approaches and discussing the thinking that underpins their use.

In your role you will be having professional conversations with beginning teachers. In order to make these conversations effective, Chapter 5 will suggest ways of focusing and deepening these conversations to enhance learning.

As a first order practitioner your subject knowledge for teaching is a significant feature of your practice. Teacher educators often have the role of nurturing the development of subject knowledge for teaching of their trainees. This is the focus of Chapter 6. Ways to develop a deep understanding of subject knowledge for teaching are suggested, which enable teachers to transform their knowledge in a variety of ways to make it accessible to their pupils.

The last four chapters focus on specific aspects of second order practitioner work and may therefore take you into new territory. Developing the professional knowledge and skills of trainees to become outstanding teachers is the aim of all teacher educators. This will help them to meet and go beyond the professional standards. Chapter 7 will enable you to identify the right mix of support and challenge to facilitate your trainees to be the best they can be. Chapter 8 helps you to nurture trainees as they face the demands of becoming a teacher.

Finally, in the last two chapters the role of research is discussed in developing high quality teacher education. In Chapter 9 you will be able to consider how you can help your trainees to draw on current research and educational theories as you develop your own practice in this field. Chapter 10 identifies arguments for research-informed practice and for developing teachers as change agents in their classrooms by undertaking small-scale research projects.

For your reflection

Figure 1.3   Reflecting on your professional development

Further reading

- Bates, T., Swennen, A. and Jones, K. (2010) *The Professional Development of Teacher Educators*. Abingdon: Routledge.
  This is a special edition of the journal *Professional Development in Education* containing a collection of papers about the professional development of teacher educators.

- Boyd, P., Harris, A. and Murray, J. (2011) *Becoming a Teacher Educator: Guidelines for Induction*. Subject Centre for Education, ESCalate: The Higher Education Academy.
  These are useful guidelines for teacher educators based mainly in higher educational institutions or further education. Included is a useful list of references relating to the professional development of teacher educators.

2

A whole school approach to professional development

Mike Stevens

This chapter covers:

- whole school professional development;
- the roles and responsibilities of teacher educators in schools;
- how we identify their impact.

What does professional development look like in a school?

It is important for you as a teacher educator to be able to recognise and share with trainees the wider context of your school's objectives for professional development and their origins. All schools have to consider a range of needs when addressing the issue of professional development. The paramount considerations are the impact on learning and teaching and on improving standards (see Figure 2.1). The impact of national and local initiatives on the school's priorities for development need to be considered so that trainees understand the bigger picture and the factors influencing education and the school's development plan.

CPD in school includes various strands that Bolam (1993) has described as professional training, professional education and professional support. Professional training may refer to subject specific areas such as subject knowledge or strategies or perhaps leadership-based training; professional education may involve longer-term courses leading to higher degrees or diplomas or small-scale enquiry into current practice; and professional support may include support from colleagues, outside agencies or local authority advisers or consultants. Trainee teachers may be involved in each strand of professional development, for example: participating in subject development within the school; enquiry into an aspect of learning; and conversations with external specialists to understand their role. CPD objectives in a school's policy may include:

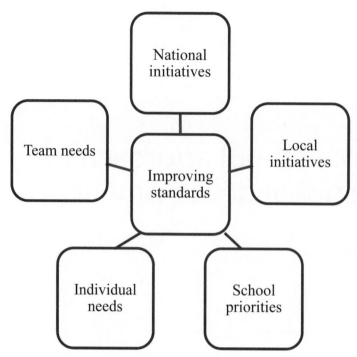

Figure 2.1   Overview of influences on professional development in school

- raising standards of achievement;
- improving the quality of leadership and management;
- improving the quality of learning and teaching;
- providing opportunities for professional development and supporting career aspirations;
- maximising the potential of the appraisal system.

The school will be able to identify opportunities in the three broad areas of professional development described above.

Who are teacher educators in schools?

Teacher educators in schools take on responsibility for the training and development of those who are entering the profession at the initial stage (trainees), those who are new to the profession (NQTs) or those who, at various stages of their careers, require support and guidance to enable them to develop and flourish professionally.

In some schools the overall responsibility for and co-ordination of professional development falls to a senior and highly experienced teacher who is usually a member of the senior leadership team, such as a deputy or the headteacher. This role, often referred to as professional mentor, is pivotal in formulating, developing and leading the quality and vision of teacher education within the school.

Other roles include those such as subject tutors or teacher mentors who take the responsibility for the day-to-day training and support of trainee teachers and NQTs.

These are all essential roles in developing good quality teacher education and early professional development. Often curriculum leaders, subject leaders or advanced skills teachers have roles as teacher educators.

A **professional mentor** supports teacher mentors in their professional development. The broad nature of this role requires good interpersonal skills, knowledge of current developments and practice and the ability to lead learning and set the standard in whole-school expectations. Successful professional mentors will have many of the following features embedded in their practice:

- formulating policy;
- selecting and de-selecting teacher mentors;
- co-ordinating or leading induction for emerging mentors and appropriate support and guidance for established mentors;
- regular and effective liaising with higher education institutions and their representatives;
- establishing and promoting effective partnership with local networks and school cluster groups;
- regular, timetabled meetings with mentors and trainees;
- assuring quality and consistency of whole school standards and expectations, from trainees to established mentors;
- overviewing timetables and workload;
- conducting lesson observations and providing formative feedback;
- providing training for lesson observations in the school context;
- encouraging reflective practice;
- ensuring good record keeping and documentation throughout the process.

Where professional mentors are well established, there is often a strong link with local partnerships and initial teacher education providers. The best of these demonstrate a close, collaborative ethos where aspects of planning, training and sharing of good practice between schools and higher education institutions are readily apparent. In such contexts, professional mentors can play a vital part in the initial recruitment of trainees and have a major role in their subsequent training and induction into the teaching profession.

It is clear that those who have responsibility for leading and developing whole school professional development have both a complex and challenging role in formulating policy and translating this into practice by ensuring that priorities which are identified in the school development plan are owned by the school's workforce and that they match development needs at every level. These priorities should be related to success criteria so that their impact can be identified.

Sharing this vision needs to be undertaken transparently in the school's policy. In this policy ways in which the school will support the development of its staff will be identified. In this way, as Hargreaves (2007) points out, the school becomes a professional learning community and may often be working effectively with other schools in 'cluster groups' to promote sustainable school improvement (Stoll et al., 2006).

The role of a **teacher mentor** is a challenging but rewarding one. It is a hands-on job which requires confidence in your own practice, and the ability to reflect and engage others in reflection. In a thriving and successful school community there is always the potential among its professional body of teachers to identify and develop those who could take on the responsibility of teacher mentor. The very nature of this role presupposes an interest in working closely with colleagues to develop and improve practice. These roles in secondary schools can be undertaken by those with subject responsibility, such as heads of department or curriculum leaders, and at primary level by experienced class teachers.

As a teacher mentor your areas of work and focus may include:

- day-to-day pastoral care of your trainee or NQT;
- regular meetings with your line-manager (professional mentor);
- establishing meeting times with your trainee;
- developing a training agenda focusing on reflection and improvement;
- modelling good practice in learning, teaching and leadership;
- observing lessons and giving formative feedback;
- undertaking professional conversations including reflection and evaluation ;
- using video recording to enhance reflection and feedback;
- monitoring and tracking subject knowledge acquisition;
- monitoring the quality of trainees' documentation;
- identifying opportunities for obtaining evidence towards the Teachers' Standards;
- working closely with partnership providers and attending training events.

In recent years, with the demands of increased accountability, quality assurance and the measurement of impact, schools have invested greater resources into the careful selection and subsequent professional development of teacher educators at this level. In many cases schools have identified and established transparent and rigorous criteria for the appointment to roles such as these because of the level of personal and professional commitment required. In best practice, opportunities for 'growing' teacher educators will be identified through the school's CPD policy and school development plan and will be matched to the needs of the school as a whole.

 Activity 2.1

Identifying your own professional development needs

Arrange to have a professional conversation with the leader of professional development in your school to explore the current priorities for professional development and how you fit in to the bigger picture in your role as a mentor. Together identify colleagues who have similar responsibilities to you and look at ways that you could share good practice e.g. doing joint observations and feedback to share approaches.

Performance management and teacher educators

Performance management (DfE, 2012) is the appraisal system adopted by most schools in England and Wales. In schools where teacher education is given high priority, performance management can be employed as a useful tool to identify impact and further invest in the training process. Good performance management which incorporates defined success criteria can help drive and improve practice and give weight and credibility to your work as a teacher educator.

If you are a new or experienced mentor, your role will be demanding and it is a good idea to identify with your line-manager key areas of focus for your continued development in the role. This could take the form of a performance management objective which may well be supported by areas identified in the school development plan. By doing this you will engage in dialogue throughout the annual cycle about your own progress in the role and about ways in which the school may further invest in you and in the work you do. For this reason, it is important to reflect on and identify the impact of what you do as teacher educator. Table 2.1 is an example of a performance management objective.

Table 2.1 A performance management objective

Focus area	Objective	Success criteria	Evidence these areas
Professional development: Teacher mentor	To mentor GTP trainee through the year	Trainee successfully completes course Trainee becomes confident practitioner Motivated and engaged pupils	• Attend training sessions • Meet weekly with trainee • Observe trainee • Assess against standards • Video recording of trainee for reflection • Maintain documentation rigorously • Lead sessions with other mentors • Share good practice

It is clear that where a school has invested resources in the professional development of its staff, and where strong partnerships between the school and higher education providers exist, opportunities will arise to nurture good mentors.

For your reflection

Who are the key people who support you in your role as a mentor?

How will you share your professional development needs with your school leadership team?

Figure 2.2 Reflecting on school aspects of your professional development

Further reading

- Bubb, S. and Earley, P. (2010) *Helping Staff Develop in Schools*. London: Sage. This is a very practical handbook for those leading professional development of staff in school. It covers identifying needs and planning for, and evaluating, impact.

- Hargreaves, D. H. (2008) *Leading System Redesign*: iNet available at https://www. ssatrust.org.uk/innovation/fellows This is a useful article that makes comparison between former and recent approaches to CPD.

3

Becoming a teacher educator: developing a new aspect to your identity

Joy Jarvis

This chapter covers:

- how to develop your identity as a teacher educator;
- building on your skills and attributes;
- how to develop expertise in engaging with research, teaching adults and leading learning.

How you identify yourself professionally and how others see you will be a significant part of your new role. While helping trainees to develop their identity as teachers you will need to consider your own identity as a 'teacher educator'. How does this new identity fit with the teacher identity you will have held for some time? You will already have identities in your school, such as subject or year leader; as a teacher and colleague who is for example: 'calm', 'sensible', 'enthusiastic' or 'motivating'. How will you be seen in your new role and how will you see yourself? So, for example, if you are organising groups of pupils in the school hall are you doing this as a teacher or are you modelling this process for trainees? You could argue that you may well be doing both, but how will it be viewed by others? Or, if you are talking in the staff room about a problem you had earlier with a pupil are you modelling ways of thinking as a teacher or are you letting off steam? As a teacher educator your own practice will be subject to scrutiny and open for discussion in a way that may not have happened since you first started teacher education yourself. It is important therefore to explore these issues and consider how you will respond to the challenges that may arise as you take on a new aspect to your identity.

Considering this topic is important because as Wenger (1998:149) suggests: 'There is a profound connection between identity and practice . . . practice entails the negotiation of ways of being a person in that context'. Your professional identity relates partly to the physical context you are in, which has not changed. You are still in your school setting, although you may also be working in wider contexts, such as connecting with teacher educators in other schools and in higher education settings. This will present challenges that are both similar and different from those facing teacher educators who move into new contexts when they take up their new roles. Research undertaken by the editors of this book, and by a significant number of others in this professional field, has tended to focus on challenges to teachers moving into higher education as this has, until now, been the usual process for those becoming teacher educators. A pattern of responses to the new role has been identified and it will be interesting for you to consider how these relate to your own perceptions.

 Activity 3.1

Make a list of the challenges that you perceive in relation to taking on a teacher educator identity.

In relation to research in this field, including our own (Chivers et al., 2010), challenges that have been identified include: feeling isolated, lacking confidence, being anxious about 'modelling' practice, being uncertain about teaching adults and being unclear about how to link practice with research. Anticipating that trainees would expect teacher educators to be knowledgeable about research and how to link with the current research agenda may be a particular anxiety for teacher educators not working in universities and for this reason we have included two chapters (9 and 10) on this topic. The idea of moving from being an expert as a teacher to being a novice as a teacher educator can be unsettling for an experienced professional. It is helpful, therefore to identify your existing strengths and what you are bringing to your new role.

 Activity 3.2

Identify the skills, attributes and values that you anticipate will contribute to your new role.

You may well have identified your experience and expertise as giving you a deep understanding of learning and may have included aspects such as communication skills, the ability to build relationships with a diverse range of people, skills in operating in uncertain and changing contexts, a level of professional confidence and an ability to be reflective on your own practice and that of others. Additionally your values and beliefs are likely to include an ethic of care and responsibility for others as well as the role of a teacher in enabling the learning of others. Two teacher educators writing about their transition from being teachers noted, '. . . our current role as teacher educators does not place us in a strange, new category of educator . . . our evolving identity as a teacher has remained with us' (Young and Erickson, 2011:

127). It is important to use and build on your current experience and expertise, while acknowledging and developing new aspects to your identity. We will discuss three aspects of your new identity which appear from research and experience to be important for teacher development: engaging with research, teaching adults and taking a leadership role.

Engaging with research

Teachers, and indeed other professionals, may have a somewhat ambivalent attitude to research. As new professionals they may well have felt a disjuncture between research based theory and what they experienced in practice. The notion of the 'ivory tower' of academia and the 'real world' of practice can become entrenched and prevent professionals engaging with literature in the field. As a teacher educator you will need to help trainees to bridge what may be perceived as the gap between theory and practice. It can be helpful to explain to trainees that all of us work from theories, whether or not they can be articulated, and that these will drive the way we teach. Looking at the work undertaken by others, particularly those who have published their research findings, enables us to ask a wide range of questions about practice. It is part of engaging in a critical reflection on practice which will be an essential process in trainees being able to develop as teachers beyond their immediate context. The following comments by teacher educators identify that this aspect of their work becomes more important as they become experienced in this role: 'I really want them to think more deeply about the bigger picture and be critical . . .' (McKeon and Harrison, 2010: 35) and 'Reading starts to feed into your practice and into what we tell the students' (Griffiths et al., 2010: 251).

Chapter 10 explores how you may engage in research yourself. You may find it useful to work with other new teacher educators to explore your developing identity and expertise in your new role, for example. This would not only add to knowledge in the field but would extend your ability to articulate your theory and practice, which would be helpful in your work with trainees. Your trainees themselves will probably be expected to undertake forms of enquiry as part of their practice development and having recent or concurrent experience of doing this yourself will enable you to help them more effectively.

Supporting trainees to research in their practice context will involve you helping them to gain multiple perspectives through drawing on literature and on knowledge from colleagues and pupils. Approaches to reading are discussed in Chapter 9. Trainees may also collect data in school from members of staff and from pupils, and helping them to do this ethically and appropriately will be part of your role as a teacher educator. Useful texts in this field are referenced in Chapter 10 and other texts may be recommended by colleagues from higher education contexts who are working with you. A key part of your work is likely to be helping trainees identify their assumptions about the topic they are researching and enabling them to question these. For example, simplistic notions about concepts of 'ability' can be questioned by reading examples of teachers' work described and explained in the text by Hart et al. (2004). Texts like this, which include a discussion of concepts and give examples of what related practice might look like, can enable trainees to understand the thinking underpinning practice.

Identifying the perspectives of others working in different school contexts can enable trainees to see that their own ways of understanding the context are not the only way. Collecting data from colleagues and pupils can be undertaken through spoken or written forms, through asking them to draw pictures or to take photographs of aspects of school life. Autobiographical texts and fiction based on experiences of learners can also enable trainees to 'decentre' and consider the classroom from the perspective of the pupil. The novel, *The Curious Incident of the Dog in the Night-Time* (Haddon, 2003) for example, written as if in the voice of a young person with Asperger's syndrome, can enable readers to understand that there are different ways of interpreting and responding to events. Reasons behind behaviour that may seem 'odd' can be more easily understood.

Our own research with trainees, Jarvis and Iantaffi (2006) and Jarvis and Trodd (2008), suggests that encouraging them to create a fictional account, based on research into children's experiences, can enable them to gain a new perspective on the classroom and as one student involved in this activity reported, 'I will never again make the naïve presumption that the way in which I see the world is the only way in which the world can be seen' (Jarvis and Iantaffi 2006: 82).

Listening to pupils and gaining feedback from them on aspects of practice can be a powerful form of learning for both trainees and teacher educators and facilitating this can be a powerful part of your teaching role. This role will be considered further in the next section.

Teaching adults

Teachers who are very confident in their role working with children and young people, may initially be less sure about their teaching role with adults as they take on their teacher educator identity. While research suggests that for the trainee teacher a key influence on his or her practice will be the personal experience of being taught, this is likely to be the same for the new teacher educator. Your experience on your own initial teaching course may lead you to feel that you need to teach in a particular way. Case studies of new teacher educators (Clemans et al., 2010) suggest that as with beginning teachers they move from a teacher-focused to a learner-focused pedagogy over time. Quotations from their case studies show how teachers learned to work effectively with teacher colleagues in a professional development role drawing on their experience as teachers (see Figure 3.1).

The idea of critical reflection, discussed earlier in the section on research, is important for all teachers at whatever stage in their professional career. Brookfield (1995) suggests that the four lenses we need to look through in order to be critically reflective are: our own experience as learners and teachers; the eyes of our pupils or trainees; our colleagues' experiences; and theoretical literature. We also discuss this further in Chapter 4. Enabling adults to develop their teaching will involve helping them to use these lenses effectively. You can suggest to trainees that they explore their own biographies to identify why they may have emotional attachment or aversion to particular ways of learning. You can demonstrate ways of gaining opinions from pupils through showing how you do this in your own practice. In addition to observing your trainees' teaching you can enable them to observe you

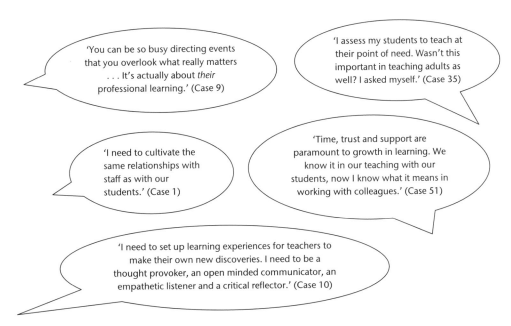

Figure 3.1 Comments of teachers leading professional development (from Clemans et al., 2010)

and your colleagues and to share feedback and perspectives. As suggested above, you can connect these experiences to relevant literature. A useful, recent text on teaching in all phases of education is *The Power of Pedagogy* by Leach and Moon (2008), which draws together a wide range of ideas in learning and teaching. It would be useful reading in order to enable both teacher educators and trainees to connect with ideas in the wider field and to draw on these as they develop their own principles of practice.

So far in this chapter it has been suggested that engaging with research and teaching adults will be part of your new identity. Leadership of learning will need to become another strand. It is likely that you will already have leadership in your school so leading learning will be a development from your existing expertise.

Leading learning

As a teacher educator you will be leading the learning of trainees and may well be developing learning opportunities for new teachers in your school and for more experienced colleagues. There may be opportunities for working with trainees and teachers from other schools. All these roles involve working with adults to bring about change and development in practice. They involve engaging with mind-sets around learning and teaching and creating opportunities for trainees and colleagues to lead their own learning for future development. Leading learning involves teacher educators thinking about the future, and about pedagogy, to enable colleagues to move beyond conforming to current initiatives and to build sustainable practice.

As a leader of learning you could be involved in group contexts, such as running sessions for colleagues, or could be engaging with individuals by being a critical friend. Leading by developing your own teaching and being a reflective practitioner yourself will be important.

> Teachers . . . need to be powerful learners if they are to maintain a high level of professional performance in an occupation that has become increasingly difficult. They also need to be role models to their students as well as to the [school] community as a whole. In this sense, a teacher's capacity to learn constitutes an important form of leadership in itself. (O'Donoghue and Clarke, 2010: 93)

Seeing yourself as a leader may be a challenge to your current identity but the activities you will be engaging in will be part of the leadership of learning in your school and in the wider context of education.

Of fundamental importance to your work will be your ability to collaborate with others to build a context of trust and collegiality where genuine joint enquiry into practice can be undertaken by colleagues, trainees and pupils. In order to do this you will need a supportive context and an opportunity to connect with others in similar contexts to your own to share ideas and experiences. Your own immediate colleagues may be focusing their work solely on the learning of pupils rather than teachers. We believe you need to join or create a community of professionals, locally or online, with similar roles to yours. This can enable your voice to be heard in a wider context to enhance practice locally and nationally.

At the beginning of this chapter we suggested that you explore the challenges of a new identity and the strengths that you bring to your new role. We hope that you will feel able to embrace the new aspects of your identity with increasing confidence as you develop your role as a teacher educator in a supportive community.

For your reflection

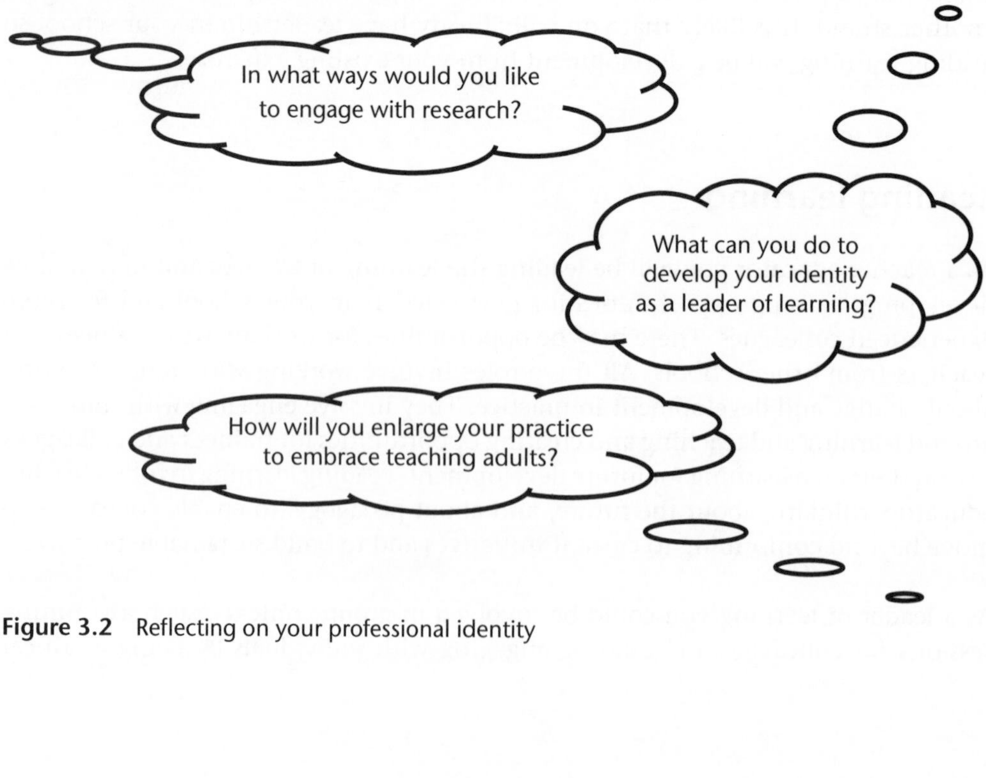

In what ways would you like to engage with research?

What can you do to develop your identity as a leader of learning?

How will you enlarge your practice to embrace teaching adults?

Figure 3.2   Reflecting on your professional identity

Further reading

- Hart, S., Dixon, A., Drummond, J. and McIntyre, D. (2004) *Learning without Limits*. Maidenhead: Open University Press.
  This book demonstrates how research findings have been implemented in classroom practice.
- Leach, J. and Moon, B. (2008) *The Power of Pedagogy*. London: Sage.
  This book explores a wide range of ideas about pedagogy that can have an impact on your practice.
- Swann, M., Peacock, A ., Hart, S. and Drummond, M.J. (2012) *Creating Learning without Limits*. Maidenhead: Open University Press.
  This text builds on the ideas explored in *Learning without Limits* and shows in detail how members of staff in one primary school worked together to enquire into and develop their practice by focusing on learning and the capacity of all children to learn.

PART B

ASPECTS OF THE PROFESSIONAL KNOWLEDGE AND PRACTICE OF TEACHER EDUCATORS

4

The pedagogy of teacher educators

Joy Jarvis and Elizabeth White

This chapter covers:

- what we know about the pedagogy of teacher educators;
- ways to model the professional knowledge and skills needed by teachers;
- how to develop your teacher educator pedagogy further.

Teacher educators instinctively believe that they should be modelling outstanding practice. Trainee teachers need to understand how experienced teachers think and the theoretical underpinning behind the choices that have been made in the classroom. This chapter looks at the challenging aspect of modelling how to teach when working with trainees, and how to make the modelling explicit. In order to understand your own practice better it is helpful to examine the personal impact of your learning experiences and to examine your professional knowledge in order to set it into the new context of meeting the needs of new teachers. Boyd and Harris (2010) suggest that teacher educators reconstruct their pedagogy during early stages of their professional development and that new teacher educators draw on their past experiences to inform their practice. In order to explore what has influenced the way you teach, the values, beliefs and theories that underpin your pedagogy, you may find it helpful to spend some time on Activity 4.1. This will enable you to consider 'who you are as a teacher' as this will have an impact on 'who you are as a teacher educator'.

 Activity 4.1

Reflect on your learning journey

1. Make a visual representation of the different times in your life where you have spent time in formal education, being taught and teaching others.
2. Identify any key experiences or people in this representation.
3. Now try to identify how these have shaped your beliefs about teaching.

Identifying the beliefs underpinning our own teaching is difficult. It is important for teacher educators to do this for two reasons: so that you can explain your own beliefs to your trainees, and so that you can help trainees to understand how their beliefs influence their practice. Your own beliefs will have been developed through experience and through discussing educational ideas and theories. One way of identifying how these relate to classroom practice is to try Activity 4.2.

 Activity 4.2

Identify your beliefs about teaching

1. Take an A5 piece of paper and represent in any way you like an **ideal** teaching session.
2. Place this in the centre of an A4 piece of paper. Using two different coloured pens identify and label (a) what the learners are doing (b) what the teacher is doing.
3. Place the A4 paper in the centre of an A3 piece of paper. Write round the edges of this paper what beliefs are represented, e.g. 'children learn best when sitting in rows', or 'children learn best when engaged in practical activities', or 'the teacher's role is to challenge pupils' ideas'.

The beliefs held about best practice may, or may not, result in action in the classroom. It is important for you as a teacher educator to consider the extent to which your practices match your beliefs as you will need to demonstrate this link to trainees when they observe you teaching. Try Activity 4.3 to help you to think about this.

 Activity 4.3

Identify how your beliefs impact on your practice as a teacher and a teacher educator

1. Make a list of what might stop you acting in the way you think is best in your classroom. What can you do to lessen their effect?
2. Draw a series of steps – on the top step write an aspect of 'ideal' practice and on the bottom step what is 'real' practice.

    For example, ideal – children choose their own level of challenge in maths activities versus real – children are given their maths challenges by the teacher.

    Write on the intermediate steps how one could move gradually from the bottom to the top step.
3. Draw a pair of spectacles and write on these your beliefs about learning and teaching so that you appreciate that these are the lenses through which you will view your trainees' practice.
4. How will your spectacles help or hinder your work as a teacher educator?

Embracing change

It may be necessary to move on in your own beliefs and practices. A good place to start is to try something different in your practice. This different behaviour can change your experiences and as a result your beliefs may change because they are shaped by experience rather than the other way around (Guskey, 2005; Russell, 2007). For example, if a new practice produces improved engagement in class and a deeper understanding of the subject, this is a positive reward, which can influence your future behaviour as well as help to mould your beliefs.

Part of your role as a teacher educator will include enabling trainees to embrace new ideas, as you introduce trainees to new practices that have been found to be effective for today's young people. This may require a change in the trainee's beliefs about how to teach. It is important to provide trainees with opportunities to understand how and why they teach in the way that they do. It is essential that trainees carry out Activities 4.1–4.3 themselves and then discuss them with each other and with you. If during this discussion you share your own results for the activities with them, this will help them to see that understanding and developing learning and teaching is an ongoing process. You will then have a better appreciation of the lenses the trainees are using to look at classroom practice.

When trainees have an appreciation of their preferred ways of teaching it may be necessary to encourage them to try out different practices, to experiment and take risks with their classes, as when they see that pupils' learning improves they will have growing confidence and belief in the new practices they are using. Modelling a willingness to experiment and take risks in your teaching will help trainees to use practices that they might not have initially believed would work. It will also help you to understand some of the challenges that your trainees are experiencing, and will help you to share the learning journey with them. Sometimes trainees will challenge your own practices and deeply held beliefs. It is important to see one of your roles as modelling ways of thinking about practice.

The most significant element in introducing new ideas into practice is not the initial training but the follow-up. When trainees start using new ideas with their classes they may have more challenging questions than when they first heard the idea. They need a continuing dialogue to help them address those issues (see Chapter 5).

Revealing how to think like a teacher

Being a teacher educator involves some distinctive pedagogical skills that differ from being a teacher and this is a crucial area for the professional development of new teacher educators. A key aim of teacher educators is facilitating learning through modelling good practice, as the teacher educator is in a position to have a strong impact on the trainees' views of teaching. Modelling is 'intentionally displaying certain behaviour with the aim of promoting trainees' professional learning' (Lunenberg et al., 2007: 589). This should not be restricted to being a good role model for trainees to observe our professional practices, but includes articulating our professional knowledge by explaining how teachers think. This is explicit modelling and could be described as 'revealing our thought bubble'.

In our experience the metacognitive process of explicit modelling contributes to the professional development of the trainees and improves our own teaching as it reduces 'unthinking practice'. Making hidden professional knowledge explicit to trainees is vital to linking practice with theory. This can be lacking when trainees are observing experienced teachers who may not articulate their professional knowledge or link their practice to educational theories.

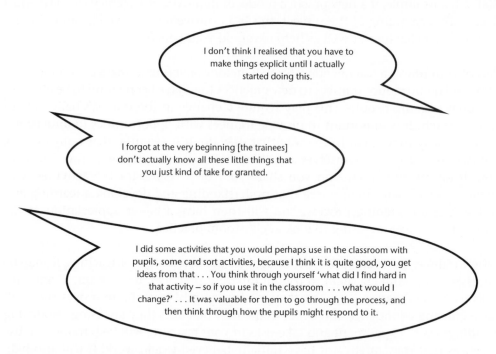

Figure 4.1   New teacher educators share their experiences of teaching trainees

New teacher educators share their experiences of teaching trainees in Figure 4.1. They illustrate by their comments that they have a growing realisation that explicit modelling is needed for trainees to learn. The following activities are practical ways to develop explicit modelling as a pedagogical tool.

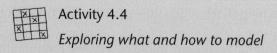   Activity 4.4

Exploring what and how to model

1. Make a list of the different aspects of your practice as a teacher which you will be modelling to your trainees.
    Example: how to organise group work.
2. Go through your list and consider how you could model each aspect to your trainees. *For example, you may be able to model a way of organising group work by (1) using group work during a session with your trainees, or (2) providing the trainees with an opportunity to observe group work during a lesson.*
3. Now look through the professional standards used in your context (in England this is the Teachers' Standards, DfE, 2011) to see if there are more aspects of your professional practice that you have overlooked on your list. It is not just the 'teaching' aspect of our work that is being modelled!

Activity 4.5

Learn from other teacher educators

1. Teachers Media has a series of lectures by teacher educators (The Teachers TV ITE Lectures Series) where you can observe other teacher educators to consider how they are modelling their practice.
2. Start by observing these two lectures:
   http://www.teachersmedia.co.uk/videos/pedagogy
   http://www.teachersmedia.co.uk/videos/creative-teaching
3. While you are observing, note the different aspects of practice that are being modelled. Think about how they are being modelled – implicitly or explicitly, alone or with a colleague, demonstration, role play etc. Can you use some of these ideas to develop your own modelling when teaching your trainees?

Although there is a need to enthuse trainees and be able to explain your personal pedagogical choices, it is important to remember that you are not creating self-replicas and they may make other choices due to their personal experiences and the contexts in which they are working. What follows are some ideas that experienced teacher educators have found useful in sharing their 'thought bubble' with their trainees:

- thinking aloud during sessions that you are leading;

- sharing lesson plans and your reasoning;

- being observed teaching lessons and later discussing the thinking behind them;

- articulating when things go wrong in a session – asking for reasons and solutions;

- linking examples to different educational contexts that your trainees might experience.

This is not a comprehensive list – you may well be able to add ideas of your own.

Enacting a pedagogy that prepares trainees for working in diverse settings

As a teacher educator you are preparing your trainees for a wide variety of educational contexts. An understanding of the cognitive processes that underpin learning is essential for teaching. Many teachers are concerned about having accurate subject knowledge in relation to the curriculum. Having an understanding of the reflective processes and metacognition that enables learning to take place is equally important. One model of teaching is delivering subject knowledge in preparation for examinations. This model is sometimes used in lectures where information is presented, but has limited scope for active learning.

We believe that effective learning in schools embraces social constructivism. (For more information on learning theories, including Vygotsky's social constructivism, see Further Reading.) This requires the learners to interact with the material, discuss with peers and learn collaboratively. Teachers are facilitators who provide a safe and challenging learning environment, where learners can verbalise their ideas and reconstruct them with others and where they can develop the confidence and language to explain what they are learning. In this way they can develop the skills required to become independent learners.

If particular methods are used to teach trainees, they may follow this model as they teach their classes. The challenge then is to ensure that you have chosen pedagogy to meet the learning purpose.

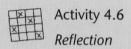 Activity 4.6

Reflection

Think back over a session that you have led with your trainees.

1. How much was led by you and how much was trainee-led?
2. What strategies did you model? How did you make them explicit?
3. What opportunities were there for dialogue and learning with peers?
4. How did you expect this session to have an impact on their practice?
5. How did you provide opportunity for reflection and evaluation of their learning and application from the session?

How to critique, develop and articulate uses of modelling in your setting

Ways that you can develop your practice include:

- peer observation;
- joint planning;
- co-teaching and reflection;
- trainee feedback;
- personal reflection.

A number of teacher educators have carried out self studies of their own practice, identifying the challenges they have found in enacting and articulating their pedagogy (see Further Reading). These include the feeling of vulnerability and the complexity of knowing when would be an appropriate time to be 'thinking aloud' and the reaction of trainees to teaching in this way (see also Chapter 3). It is vital to have a responsive relationship with your trainees and to develop an on-going dialogue with them that includes listening to their feedback on how they are experiencing your teaching. Russell (2007: 182) states that 'creating and sustaining a teaching-learning relationship with each student is now the fundamental goal from which all else follows'. He used 'tickets out of class' (Russell, 2007: 184) to collect comments. Face to face or online discussions with trainees following sessions can produce direct feedback and give opportunities to make your thinking explicit to trainees. Using a variety of feedback strategies can help to develop communication within the learning community.

For your reflection

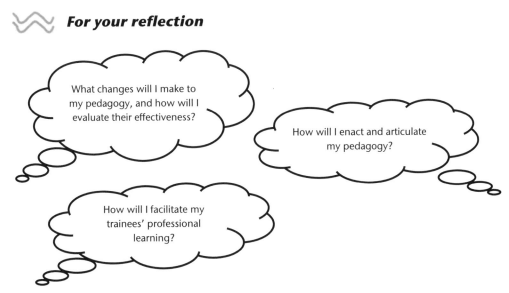

Figure 4.2   Reflecting on your pedagogy

Further reading

Useful books relating to developing the pedagogy of teacher educators:

- Loughran, J. (2006) *Developing a Pedagogy of Teacher Education: Understanding Teaching and Learning about Teaching.* London: Routledge.
- Raths, J. and McAninch, A. (2003) *Teacher Beliefs and Classroom Performance: The Impact of Teacher Education.* Greenwich: Information Age Publishing.
- Russell, T. and Loughran, J. (eds) (2007) *Enacting a Pedagogy of Teacher Education. Values, Relationships and Practices.* Abingdon: Routledge.

Research including self-studies of new teacher educators:

- Boyd, P. and Harris, K. (2010) Becoming a university lecturer in teacher education: expert school teachers reconstructing their pedagogy and identity. *Professional Development in Education*, 36: 9–24.
- Loughran, J. and Berry, A. (2005) Modelling by teacher educators. *Teaching and Teacher Education*, 21: 193–203.
- White, E. (2011) Working towards explicit modelling: experiences of a new teacher educator. *Professional Development in Education*, 37: 483–98.

Learning theories and their application for training teachers for today's schools:

- Alexander, R. (2008) *Towards Dialogic Teaching.* Cambridge: Dialogos.

- Atherton, J. S. (2011) Learning and Teaching: Angles on learning, particularly after the schooling years [online: UK] from http://www.learningandteaching. info/learning/index.htm

- Fisher, A., Russell, K., MacBlain, S., Purdy, N., Curry, A. and MacBlain, A. (2010) Re-examining the culture of learning in ITE: Engaging with the new demands of the 21st century. *Critical and Reflective Practice in Education*, 2: 92–102.

5

Enhancing professional learning conversations

Sally Graham

> ## This chapter covers:
>
> - professional learning conversations with trainees and new colleagues;
> - a 3D approach to structuring these conversations;
> - an example of what this might look like in practice.

You will have many formal and informal conversations about learning with your trainees and colleagues. This chapter explores the planned conversations you will have on an individual basis with trainees or new colleagues about learning and teaching. In these conversations you will be drawing on your abilities to establish relationships, through trust and understanding, in order to communicate effectively. You will be creating a context that will enable a trainee or colleague to reflect on, and learn from, experience. This will then lead to action being taken for professional development.

Before looking closely at a process you might use to undertake these professional learning conversations it would be useful to reflect yourself on your own reactions to teaching events.

 Activity 5.1

Personal reflections

1. List some words that you associate with how you respond when one of your lessons has gone well.
2. Now do the same with a lesson that went less well.

You may find that you have identified words describing emotions; we often talk about the highs and lows of teaching. It is important to remember that teaching is an emotional activity and that trainees may well be experiencing extremes; times when they think teaching is wonderful and times when they wonder why they ever decided to enter this profession! As Maynard and Furlong (1995: 10) have noted, learning to teach can be a 'complex, bewildering and sometimes painful task'. Trainees are likely to be challenged in relation to their concept of themselves as a competent adult and to need reassurance that they have the resources to do the job as they would like it to be done. As you will know from interactions with colleagues and pupils there is need for a balance between encouragement and questioning, between support and challenge. As a teacher you may feel that you should identify issues with their teaching for trainees and find a solution for them. Experience over many years suggests, however, that in the long term it is more effective to enable trainees to work through a reflective process and to identify their own solutions. In this chapter, therefore, we offer an approach that you may find enables you to support trainees to reflect, learn and plan; a process that they can then use in their future careers.

The approach suggested here has been developed and researched by a team of teacher educators, initially with newly qualified teachers and more recently with trainees (Graham et al. in preparation). We will draw on some of the staff and student responses to this approach later in this chapter. The aim of the process was to enable participants to:

- reflect upon their professional practice, identifying professional development needs;

- reflect through personal enquiry upon the nature and extent of their professional development against relevant professional standards;

- develop and sustain confidence in their professional expertise and increase their autonomy in terms of their professional development.

Two key concepts underpinned the creation of the approach: reflection and critical moments. Mezirow's (1990) two levels of reflection were seen as important. Reflection can lead to problem solving while critical reflection, the process suggested here, leads to a critique of underlying assumptions. 'By far the most significant learning experiences in adulthood involve critical self-reflection – reassessing the way we have posed problems and reassessing our own orientation to perceiving, knowing, believing, feeling and acting' (Mezirow, 1990: 4). We are aiming for the trainees not only to deal with immediate issues but also to gain a wider and deeper perspective on teaching in order to develop more informed, principled practice.

Critical moments, or incidents which stand out in the memory as being significant, can be useful starting points for reflection where *we can best confront the values and beliefs that underpin our thinking, perception and action* (Francis, 1997: 171). Trainees will be documenting teaching experiences and will bring these with them to the conversation with you in your role as a teacher educator.

Finding a space

Finding a physical space for professional learning conversations may not be easy, nor may it be simple to find a time when you and your trainee can meet. It is important, however, to schedule both space and time for this activity as it can be one of the most important learning experiences for the trainee. Investment in these conversations can mean that the trainee becomes more independent and needs less support in the future. You will already have many of the skills and qualities needed to undertake a learning conversation, as you will see through undertaking Activity 5.2.

Activity 5.2
Skills and qualities

Identify which of these skills and qualities you feel you have and those which you may be less confident in using:

- listening;
- building rapport;
- being in the moment;
- noticing;
- demonstrating empathy;
- questioning;
- paraphrasing;
- reflecting back;
- summarising;
- being open to new ideas;
- challenging;
- confronting.

You are likely to be more comfortable with using some of these than others and, of course, the judgement about when to use which approach can only be made in relation to the particular context. What is important is that you become more conscious of the skills you have and identify when you are using them. This will enable you to act more knowingly in the midst of the conversation and to make deliberate choices about what would be the most effective approach to use.

Discover – Deepen – Do (The 3D Approach)

The 3D approach was designed to drive change in teaching through reflection on critical moments (see Figure 5.1).

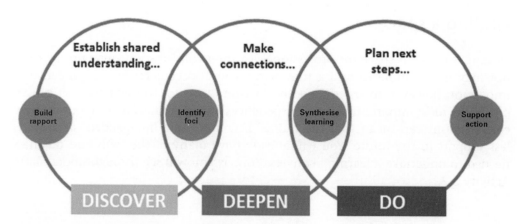

Figure 5.1   The 3D approach

- Discover – identify critical moments from practice.

- Deepen – gain greater understanding of the issues involved through making new connections and gaining new perspectives. This can be undertaken by critical reflection with colleagues and teacher educators, and by engaging in enquiry into practice and relevant literature.

- Do – set targets to make changes to practice to embed these new ideas.

In one session you might take a quarter of the time discovering a shared focus, half the time deepening understanding and the final quarter identifying and planning for action. Supporting the action would follow on from the conversation and would involve you in arranging with the trainee how this would happen. The next learning conversation might have a different or connected focus depending on the issues raised by the trainee. The activities that you would undertake during the different stages of the learning conversation are identified in Figure 5.2.

One of the challenges you may face using this approach is the desire to give advice and find solutions to problems, rather than stepping back, waiting and supporting the trainee to identify a way forward. This does not mean that you do not intervene, but the intervention is more helpful if it is focused questions which enable the trainee to notice what you may have already identified as an issue. So, layering of questions may enable you to support the trainee's reflection. For example:

- Why do you think the pupils didn't engage with the activity?
- What evidence have you that it was because they weren't interested?
- Could you identify other reasons why they might have difficulty engaging?
- What might you look for in their behaviour?
- How else might you find out why they didn't engage?

An example of using the 3D approach

Below is an outline of a fictional professional learning conversation undertaken using the 3D approach. A fictional scenario allows the drawing together of key

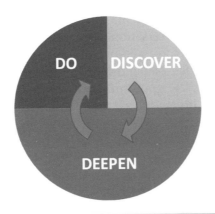

DISCOVER	DEEPEN	DO
• create mutual openness and trust • be attentive and listen • show respect • be patient and caring • create a positive environment • show empathy • exhibit a sense of sharing	• ask open questions • don't make assumptions, be non-judgemental • offer feedback through summarising, paraphrasing and further questioning • make links between theory and practice • share insights and hunches	• identify next stages to take the learning forward • establish a vision for the future • set targets • critically reflect on insights gained and any new connections made • identify patterns of behaviour • promote and support change • identify measures of success

Figure 5.2 Activities for your professional learning conversation

aspects from different conversations and allows ethical issues around confidentiality to be managed. A similar approach is used by Campbell and Kane (1998) in their text *School Based Teacher Education: Tales from a Fictional Primary School*. In this book they create stories of trainees and their mentors drawn from data collected during a research project on mentoring in schools. These stories allow issues to be identified and for teacher educators in schools to connect with examples and relate them to their own experience. You may find this an interesting book to explore in relation to your own practice.

The example we are using here is of Steve, a trainee, and Nadia, his teacher educator, who is also a subject leader in her school. Steve is an enthusiastic, energetic teacher who aims to engage his pupils in active learning. He wants them to be creative problem solvers and to work together to explore learning activities. Recently he set up a carousel of activities, with written instructions and formats for pupils to record their findings. He was disappointed that the session seemed to be, in his words, 'chaos'. He found that many pupils were not using the equipment provided appropriately, and that while some were trying the activities others were wandering round the room. It is this session and his feelings of disappointment that he brings to the professional learning conversation.

Discover: In the first instance, Nadia listens to Steve talk about this example over a cup of tea. She also takes the opportunity of reminding him of more successful lessons he has done so that his emotional response to one session does not dominate the exchange. She also positions what happened as an example of practice to be explored, rather than as a personal failure, which is how Steve perceives the session. Positioning learning to teach as an enquiry can help to depersonalise the situation so that a joint enquiry between the trainee and the teacher educator, or between groups of trainees and colleagues, becomes more possible. Knowing that there is not one way of acting, but rather a range of possibilities that can be tried, can allow the trainee to choose a way forward that seems appropriate in the circumstances, but could be changed when new insights become available. Professional actions are always created in response to particular situations and people, and as Usher et al. (1997: 130) argue, 'The question which always faces the practitioner – How ought I to act? – does not have an invariant answer'. Individuals make sense of a situation and take professional decisions in the light of the way they construe the situation. Nadia asks questions to clarify a specific focus for the discussion and moves Steve on from assumptions such as 'the pupils aren't mature enough to work this way', and 'I think I will have to do more formal teaching as I can't do activity learning'. She asks him to imagine he is a named pupil and describe the lesson from his perspective. From this Steve identifies one pupil's viewpoint: 'Kiefer wouldn't have liked working with that group who would boss him around. I don't think he would have been assertive enough to have used the equipment.' Steve identified that he would like to explore ideas around effective group working.

Deepen: In this part of the conversation Nadia and Steve discuss experiences of group work, including sessions he has observed of hers and other sessions he has done in which the group activities were more effective. He recalls a session at the university where a group of trainees engaged in a carousel of activities which he had found 'pretty pointless' at the time but which he now realises was a 'modelling' of this type of learning from which he can recall the polite sharing of group roles among the adults involved. He decides that he needs to develop understanding of group roles and a way of allocating these. Nadia brought a short text with her on using visual support to help pupils remember. This was one of a potential bank of resources she could draw on during the conversation. They discuss this and Steve decides that he should use more pictures and not too much text when facilitating group work. Nadia helps Steve to draw together his thinking on facilitating pupils to work in groups and to move on to strategies he will use.

Do: Steve decides that together with the pupils he is going to develop characters to depict each role that needs performing in the group and to illustrate these as cartoon characters. He identifies how these roles will be explained and practised and then allocated and changed at each new activity in the carousel. He also decides that one of these roles will be that of monitoring the process of the session and reporting back to him what worked effectively, what was difficult to understand and any problems they could identify with the organisation. Nadia identifies a group work session that she will be running and invites him to observe this. She suggests that he chooses a pupil to follow through the lesson so that he can gain insight into the experience and feed back any ideas to her.

Reflection on the example of using the 3D approach

Nadia had come to the meeting with a concern that Steve was not giving clear instructions at the start of his activity carousel and was not giving pupils a way of returning to these instructions when they forgot what to do. She thought he was using too much writing in his activity explanations, which she felt many pupils were not accessing. She had brought the text on memory hoping that it would stimulate Steve to consider the way he gives and documents instructions. She notes: 'I initially found this 3D approach difficult as I wanted to tell him what to do. I could see the issues so clearly from my perspective but I had to realise that he needs to develop the problem solving process himself if he is to learn effectively. Also he had a different perspective which is certainly appropriate. His ideas are not what I would have done – however, I might try his "characters" idea myself!'

Steve was initially despondent when he came to the conversation and was wondering whether trying group activity learning was worth all the effort. However, he became energised through the deepening section of the conversation and is excited about creating cartoon characters with his pupils, an activity he thinks they will enjoy and will help with undertaking group work. He also feels confident that he can take any other issues to discuss with Nadia and that they can work on these together. He notes: 'I can see how this group work is more complicated than I thought but now I can see how to solve the problems as they arise. The cartoon characters will be fun but they won't be the answer to everything. I will get ideas from the "monitoring pupils" about issues and I will involve them in the problem solving too. We can try having learning conversations.'

How the 3D approach could work for you

When the evaluation of the initial trial of this 3D approach was undertaken a number of university tutors involved in the process noted that the 'deepening' aspect of the conversation enabled new teachers to be more 'resourceful'. New teachers noted that this was an approach they could use themselves with colleagues. Part of the development of a school as a learning community, in which colleagues work together enquiring into practice, is to enable effective professional learning conversations to take place. In your role as a teacher educator you can explore this approach with trainees and colleagues and can develop a way of working that suits your context. Developing effective professional learning conversations can be part of your leadership of learning in your own setting. As Haggarty and Postlethwaite (2012: 260) note 'teachers need to be active members of a community that supports learning and enquiry; and there needs to be a pedagogy for beginning teacher learning which moves [teacher educators] on to an informed and sophisticated level of thinking, support and activity'.

For your reflection

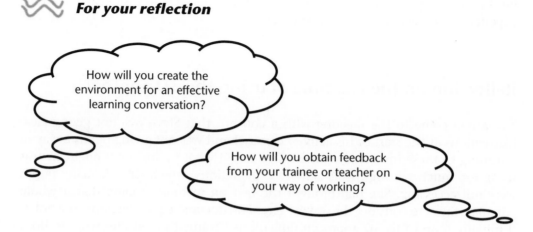

Figure 5.3   Reflecting on your professional learning conversations

📖 *Further reading*

- Relationships for Learning – University and NQTs www.teachersmedia.co.uk/videos/relationships-for-learning-university-and-nqt
  This video explores the 3D approach and how it can be used.

- Askey, S. and Carnell, E. (2011) *Transformative Coaching: A learning theory for practice.* London: Institute of Education.
  This text explores how taking a coaching approach can transform thinking and learning in practice.

- De Haan, E. and Burger, Y. (2005) *Coaching with Colleagues: An action guide for one-to-one learning.* Basingstoke: Palgrave MacMillan.
  This is a useful text giving coaching strategies that could be used to support professional learning in conversational contexts.

- Kline, N. (2001) *Time to Think: Listening to ignite the human mind.* London: Ward Lock.
  This text takes a practical approach to the use of listening to support learning.

How to nurture the development of subject knowledge for teaching

Elizabeth White

This chapter covers:

- what we know about the nature of subject knowledge;
- ways to examine your own subject knowledge;
- how to help trainees to transform their subject knowledge to make it accessible to pupils.

In developing subject knowledge our aim is to enable trainees to reason soundly and to use their knowledge base to provide the underpinning for their teaching. For primary trainees there is a broad range of subject knowledge required for teaching across the subject areas on the curriculum of their school, whereas for secondary trainees there will be a smaller range of subjects to explore in greater depth.

Imagine your trainee is standing at a particular place, A, in their understanding. In order to travel from A to B, a place that is further on in their understanding, you may give them a set of instructions for the route. This is an example of **instrumental understanding**. It requires learning and remembering a set of instructions, and reaps rapid but limited rewards. Alternatively, you may help them develop a mental map of how A relates to B so that they can work out a number of alternative routes, or you may help them to work out those routes. This is an example of **relational understanding**. It requires a deeper understanding that enables application of principles to new situations. A relational understanding of a subject leads to the trainee becoming independent of the tutor. In both these cases we have assumed that place B is a recognisable place to the trainee and the teacher educator. Another way that we might work, as teacher educators, is to challenge the trainee about B – do they know what B looks like? Does it have to be that place or could there be a better place to go? Maybe we can help them construct a picture of B that is different from what they already have. This could be called **visionary understanding** and can help develop teachers who think creatively about their own professional development, empowering them to reach their full potential.

Activity 6.1

Envisioning the endpoint of your training

Spend some time imagining what your trainees could achieve as teachers of this subject.

- What knowledge would you like them to have?
- How would you like them to teach?
- What would they know about their learners?
- What would make them outstanding teachers of this subject?
- How could you help them catch this vision of themselves?
- Are there any barriers that may impede their progress?

Capture your thoughts so that you can revisit them after you have been working with these trainees for a while.

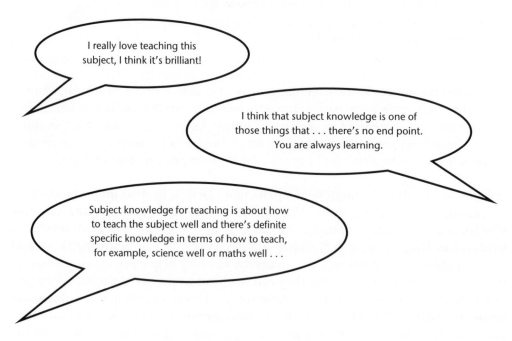

Figure 6.1   What experienced teachers say about teaching

The comments of experienced teachers (Figure 6.1), from our research (White, in preparation), reveal that there is more to subject knowledge than the content alone. The attitudes that you hold about the subject and learning are also important. As experienced teachers, our subject knowledge is complex and has developed over years of practical experience in different educational settings as well as in our academic studies. In order to disseminate your understanding and knowledge to others it is useful to deconstruct your subject knowledge into key elements. Models can be useful for this purpose. A model is a simplified version of complex interrelationships which can form a good starting place to map or audit our current subject knowledge and to draw up an action plan to develop that knowledge further or more fully. A number of models of teachers' subject knowledge can be found in the literature (see Further Reading). There is a debate about the nature of subject knowledge and what it includes. As it is important to have a shared language with which to explore subject knowledge in order to fully support trainees, we are using the subject knowledge for teaching (SKfT) framework (TDA, 2007). We have found this a helpful model to use with trainees as it is learner-centred.

'Subject knowledge for teaching' or SKfT

SKfT means more than 'subject knowledge *per se*'. It is the knowledge required by teachers, but not other subject specialists, in order to transform their subject knowledge in ways that enable others to gain a deep understanding of the concepts and skills within the subject. For example, a mathematician shares subject knowledge with a mathematics teacher. However, mathematics teachers have additional knowledge of mathematics that enables them to facilitate others to develop their mathematical skills and knowledge. The SKfT Framework (TDA, 2007) is a useful model to look at four elements of SKfT:

- Subject knowledge *per se* (**SK1**): The essential knowledge and understanding needed in order to teach a subject effectively (WHAT we know about this subject).

- Pedagogy (**SK2**) – subject theory and practice: An understanding of the teaching skills and strategies needed to teach all pupils effectively (HOW we teach this subject).

- Pupils' development (**SK3**): An understanding of how learning is linked to pupils' development and their social, religious, ethnic, cultural and linguistic backgrounds and contexts (WHEN we teach this subject).

- Attitudes (**SK4**): Positive attitudes to pupils' learning that underpin subject knowledge, skills and understanding (WHY we teach this subject).

Using this model to categorise subject knowledge into discrete areas can be useful for raising awareness of the aspects to which trainees need to attend; however, the complexity of teaching means that in reality the edge between these categories is blurred and overlapping. The following activity will help you to focus on subject specific interpretations of the elements of SKfT.

Activity 6.2

Create subject knowledge examples to use with trainees

In order to understand in more depth what we mean by **SK1**, **SK2**, **SK3** and **SK4**, consider each point in Table 6.1 and create your own examples for the subject and the age phases that you teach. The document you create will be useful to your trainees.

For example: Subject knowledge *per se*

Have an understanding of progression in the subject as defined by the National Curriculum and other national expectations
Primary English example: progression in the acquisition of phonic knowledge, linking sounds to letters and blending.

Creating a SKfT audit and action plan

Trainee teachers need to produce an audit to map the development of SKfT over their training for each of the subjects they teach. It is important not to develop a 'tick box' mentality to this audit, as this destroys creativity and engagement. The combination of SKfT audit and action plan together makes this an ongoing dynamic and personal process where trainees show progression in their understanding of the subject and how to teach it, their understanding of how pupils learn the subject and their own attitudes about the subject. The next activity is designed to stimulate your thinking about SKfT auditing and action planning.

Activity 6.3

Audit an area of your SKfT

Take a topic that you might teach in school and identify the subject knowledge needed to plan for outstanding learning and teaching in this topic. Use the four elements of the SKfT Framework (see above) to help you. Using this experience, design a way for your trainees to audit their SKfT and track their progress.

Transforming subject knowledge *per se* for your learners

It is important to recognise the steps that you use instinctively during preparation and teaching so that you can make them explicit to trainees. A way of identifying the processes involved in transforming subject knowledge *per se* (**SK1**) so that pupils can grasp new concepts and learn new skills is outlined in Table 6.2. Based on work by Shulman (1987), this includes the realisation that at the end of teaching there is new understanding for the teacher, as well as for the learners. Trainees can use their SKfT audit to record this learning and build on it through discussion with other subject specialists and their peers.

Table 6.1   A way of looking at SKfT

WHAT? **SK1** Subject knowledge *per se*	HOW? **SK2** Pedagogy
Have knowledge of the key concepts, language, skills and topics that define the subject	Make the subject accessible to pupils at different stages in their learning/development
Have knowledge of the content as defined by the National Curriculum and examination specifications	Demonstrate a range of teaching skills and strategies to promote pupils' learning in the subject
Have an understanding of progression in the subject as defined by the National Curriculum and other national expectations	Assess pupils' learning in a variety of ways and use the information to plan for subject teaching which meets pupils' needs
Identify key ideas in the subject by generalising from specific examples	Reflect on and improve teaching and learning in the subject
Have an understanding of the relationships within the subject	Respond to unexpected subject questions
Have an understanding of the relevance of the subject and why aspects of the subject are taught	Make use of a range of resources including ICT in teaching the subject
Make connections between and across subjects, including literacy, numeracy and ICT	Have high expectations of all pupils and skills to overcome barriers to their learning in the subject
Have knowledge and understanding of assessing pupils' achievement in the subject	Ask pupils appropriate subject questions
	Relate teaching of the subject to the local cultural context
WHEN? **SK3** Pupils' development	WHY? **SK4** Attitudes
Have understanding of the impact of the pupils' social, emotional and cultural development on their learning the subject	Have commitment to learning from and listening to other people, including pupils, about the subject
Have knowledge of the steps in pupils' learning of the subject	Have commitment to the inclusion, achievement and wellbeing of all pupils in the subject
Have understanding of the range of ways pupils learn the subject	Have cultural sensitivity in the subject
Ability to recognise how the subject needs to be adapted to meet pupils' individual needs and contexts	Be creative in developing learning opportunities for all pupils in the subject
Ability to recognise cognitive development as shown by misconceptions	Have enthusiasm for the subject and teaching it
Have understanding of how to overcome pupils' difficulties in learning the subject	Have commitment to continuous professional development of subject knowledge
Have understanding of how parents and carers contribute to their children's development and learning of the subject	

Table 6.2   Steps to transforming subject knowledge *per se* (**SK1**) for your learners

Personal understanding (What do I know?)
Of subject content and concepts and their relationship to other subjects (**SK1**)

TRANSFORMATION

Preparation (Why am I teaching this now?)
Critical analysis of texts, clear understanding of relationships within curriculum (**SK1**)

Representation (How can I make it clear to the learners?)
Demonstrations, analogies, explanations, examples, models, diagrams (**SK2**)

Selection (Which are the best ways for my context?)
To fit with school priorities and ethos, available resources and teaching space (**SK2**)

Personalisation (Which are the best ways for my learners?)
Aware of prior knowledge, misconceptions, backgrounds, developmental stages (**SK3**)

Teaching
Communicating, interactive teaching, managing class, assessment for learning

Evaluation (How am I doing and how well are the learners understanding?)
Monitor understanding during and after teaching (**SK3**). Evaluate own effectiveness (**SK4**)

Reflection (How can I build on this?)
Critical analysis of own and learners' performance based on evidence to inform future practice (**SK4**)

New understanding (What have I learnt?)
About myself, my learners, subject knowledge and how to teach it (**SK4**)
HOW WILL YOU CAPTURE THIS?

Activity 6.4

Transforming your subject knowledge per se (SK1) for your learners

Look at each of the steps in Table 6.2 with your trainees. Which steps do trainees find the most challenging? How could you model good practice for them in this area? Are there resources that would help them?

Identifying the needs of trainees

Trainees will identify and record some of their needs themselves through their SKfT audit. They may become aware of their needs through inspecting the National Curriculum requirements, schemes of work, Standard Assessment Test (SAT) mark schemes, examination specifications, course books and teachers' guides. When they observe other teachers, discuss with peers and colleagues and are observed teaching, other SKfT needs will emerge. The following activity uses the SKfT Framework as a tool to consider the ways subject knowledge comes into play during a lesson observation.

Activity 6.5

Observing SKfT

Before observing the lesson, agree with the trainee which element of SKfT will be the focus. Review and discuss their lesson plan well in advance of teaching. Prepare a checklist for the focus using Table 6.1. An example is provided where the focus is **SK2** (see Table 6.3).

After the observation read through your completed observation form and look for the following:

- a positive tone and constructive comments;

- subject specific comments;

- questions delving deeper into the subject matter;

- questions asking the trainee about their practice;

- advice and alternative suggestions.

Table 6.3   Observation form: focus on pedagogy **(SK2)**

Is trainee able to:	COMMENTS
• ensure that the initial presentation is clear, accurate and fluently given?	
• give clear explanation?	
• give clear instructions?	
• model what pupils have to do?	
• discuss key points?	
• involve pupils actively in the lesson?	
• ask questions which are pertinent and helpful to the pupils?	
• listen and respond appropriately to the pupils' questions?	
• draw on secure subject knowledge in answering questions?	
• ensure that explanations and tasks relate to the full range of attainment in the group?	
• demonstrate a wide repertoire of knowledge in challenging and supporting pupils?	
• select resources and strategies suitable for the subject specific content of the lesson?	
• use appropriate subject specific ICT?	
• draw the learning and attention of pupils together at the end of lesson and summarise key points?	

OVERALL COMMENTS

DEVELOPMENTAL TARGETS AND SUGGESTED ACTION POINTS

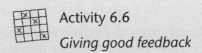

Activity 6.6

Giving good feedback

For the lesson that you observed in Activity 6.5, give feedback on the same day, face to face with the trainee. The following points will guide you:

- Ask questions to develop a two-way dialogue and promote reflective practice, e.g. how could you improve this? What other ways are there of doing this?
- Discuss implications for future lessons and planning.
- Start and end with positive aspects, and include some areas for improvement in the middle. Make sure the balance is mainly positive.

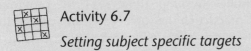

Activity 6.7

Setting subject specific targets

The nature of targets set depends on the confidence, strengths and needs of the trainee. Targets should be developed through discussion and negotiation with the trainee. Identify subject specific targets for your trainee.

Examples:
Next week, be observed explaining key words by giving some examples.

Trial some practical work and identify challenges that may occur with your pupils.

There is more about setting targets in Chapter 7.

The following characteristics may be observed where the trainee has limited SKfT:

- transmitting factual knowledge rather than facilitating engagement with the subject;
- using undemanding questioning based on recall of facts;
- avoiding open discussions of pupil ideas;
- not identifying pupil misconceptions;
- keeping to the content in course books and schemes of work.

How can SKfT be developed?

At the beginning of their training an initial needs analysis is carried out to compare the prior learning of trainees with the areas of subject knowledge they will need for teaching. This usually reveals aspects of all four elements of SKfT that will need addressing. There are three key groups of people involved in this process – the trainees, subject tutors and teacher mentors:

- **Trainees** can develop their SKfT using a range of resources including course books, internet resources, subject organisations and discussion forums.

- **Subject tutors** may help trainees develop their SKfT through creating a social environment for trainees to take risks together and become aware of their misconceptions. Modelling your continuing engagement with effective and innovative ways of learning the subject can be a powerful strategy (see Chapter 4).

- **Teacher mentors** may help trainees develop their SKfT by providing opportunities for a trainee to observe practice in the subject area and explaining the reasoning behind pedagogical decisions made when teaching the subject. Team teaching and observing trainees practice, giving feedback and setting subject specific targets are all effective ways to develop SKfT.

For your reflection

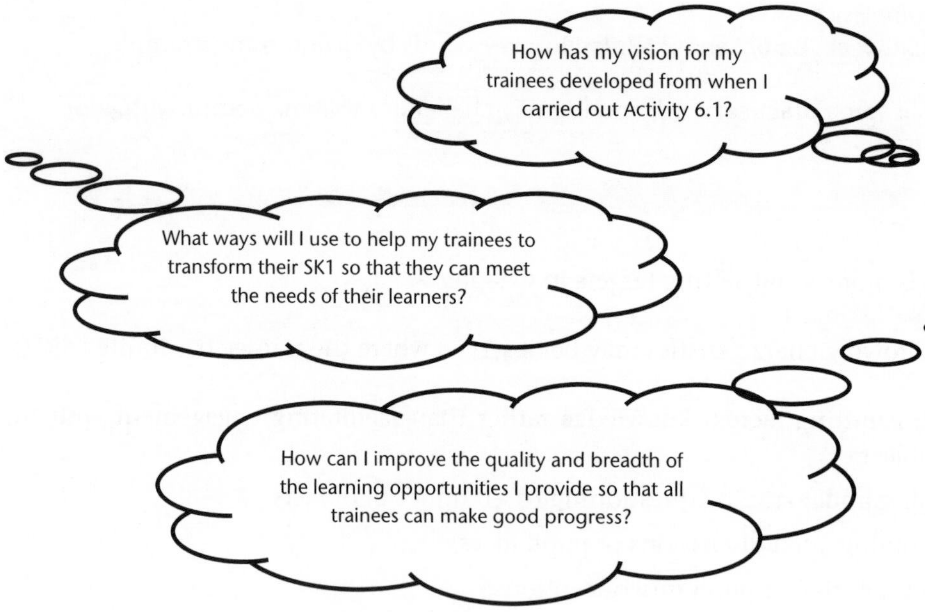

How has my vision for my trainees developed from when I carried out Activity 6.1?

What ways will I use to help my trainees to transform their SK1 so that they can meet the needs of their learners?

How can I improve the quality and breadth of the learning opportunities I provide so that all trainees can make good progress?

Figure 6.2   Reflecting on nurturing the development of SKfT

Further reading

- **Teachers Media** www.teachersmedia.co.uk
  This can be a useful website to help you develop SKfT. Search by stage and subject to provide useful video clips to illustrate aspects of teaching different subjects that you are unable to demonstrate conveniently.

- **Subject organisations** www.subjectassociation.org.uk
  You may find useful resources for your own teaching and to share with trainees through subject organisations.

- Evans, A., Hawksley, F., Holland, M. R. and Caillau, I. (2008) Improving Subject Knowledge and Subject Pedagogic Knowledge in Employment- based Secondary Initial Teacher Training in England. *Annual Conference of the Association of Teacher Education in Europe.* Vrije Universiteit Brussel. Available at: http://shura.shu.ac.uk/187/
  These authors investigated how trainee teachers acquire subject knowledge in school and have constructed a model that emphasises the dynamic nature of this process.

- Moon, B. (2006) The Subject Knowledge Debate. Available at: www.tlrp.org/themes/seminar/moon/papers.html
  Moon shows how a different model for subject knowledge has been used to help teachers analyse their subject knowledge. It features some of the aspects that are identified in the SKfT Framework.

- TDA (2007) Developing trainees' subject knowledge for teaching. A way of looking at subject knowledge for teaching. Available at: http://dera.ioe.ac.uk/9688/
  This document introduces the SKfT framework, with primary English examples. There is also a booklet for reviewing teacher training provision.

Providing the right mix of support and challenge

Phil Lenten

This chapter covers:

- the role of the teacher educator in supporting trainees in school;
- the importance of good working relationships;
- stages of mentoring.

All trainees want to use their training experience to become 'the best they can be', whatever criteria that is measured against. It is the role of teacher educators to provide the right mix of support and challenge to enable this to happen. If you are reading this as a mentor for a trainee teacher you may not have thought of yourself as a teacher educator before but this is about you and your role. In this chapter we will outline the requirements for good quality teacher training in schools with a particular focus on the central role of the mentor and how that role changes with time.

It is important to realise that you do not fulfil the requirements of your mentor role in isolation. There are 'significant others' who support both you and 'your' trainee. This will include at least one senior colleague in your school and a tutor from the training provider. The best school-based teacher training occurs where there is a culture of CPD for all staff (see Chapter 2).

The starting point in any collaboration between a mentor and trainee is the nature of the working relationship (see Figure 7.1).

This simple grid emphasises two main elements influencing the way a teacher educator and trainee work together. The right balance is obviously one where there is a reasonably high level of support and challenge.

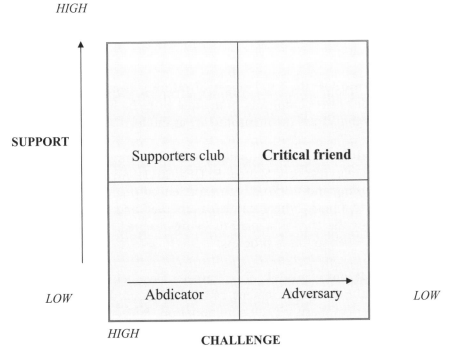

Figure 7.1 Support–challenge grid

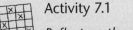 Activity 7.1

Reflect on the relationship between you and your trainee

Take a few moments to think through what Figure 7.1 has to say about the working relationship between mentor and trainee.

- What would each of these descriptors look like in practice in a school context?
- What will it mean for you to be a 'critical friend?'
- How will you avoid being too critical or too friendly?
- How will it influence the way you organise the training experience?

In the literature there are significantly differing views on the best approach to teacher training in schools. Freedman et al. (2008), for instance, argue for an apprentice style of training in the classroom with a mentor introducing a novice to the art of teaching. Whitehead and Fitzgerald (2004) promote a more open and reciprocal form of partnership with the mentor sharing in reflection in action rather than assuming a role of expert. They are critical of a model of mentoring with a hierarchy of teacher mentor as expert training an apprentice. There are many variations on these views and we want to suggest that the following models of mentoring align with our view that the relationship must change with time. Maynard and Furlong

(1993) considered three models of mentoring in their study of Initial Teacher Training. They called them the **Apprenticeship model**, the **Competency model** and the **Reflective practitioner model**. These three 'models' can be summarised as follows:

Apprenticeship model: the early stages of training need practical experience where sense is made of the complexity of the role with the help of an 'interpreter'. Collaborative teaching allows the mentor to act as model.

Competency model: the mentor provides practical training against a pre-defined set of competences (e.g. Teachers' Standards; DFE, 2011). An extended repertoire is developed by observing and working with experienced practitioners. This support structure can lead to a point where standards are 'met' and further progress slows or stops. Some describe this as a plateau being reached, a place of high-level achievement but a levelling off of progress.

Reflective practitioner model: once trainees have achieved basic classroom competence, a more dynamic element can be introduced into the mentoring process with greater emphasis on self-determination. Reflecting on teaching must be a central part of the learning process. Trainees think through different ways of teaching and develop their own justifications and practical principles from their work.

The first two models are based on the notion of trainees learning from experienced teachers and thus gaining the necessary competencies of classroom practice. Trainees seek to gain Qualified Teacher Status by providing evidence set against the Teachers' Standards, as in the competency model. The third, reflective practitioner, model is less hierarchical and anticipates a relationship based on professional dialogue where the trainee and mentor jointly explore practice to give it meaning and to identify alternative approaches (see Chapter 5). In this case the mentor is also viewed as a learner. This implied hierarchy of the three models of mentoring highlights a progression from initially making sense of the world of the classroom, to a development of a repertoire of personal competences to a fully competent, self-actualising professional. This mirrors the typical learning process for almost all of us in new situations and much the same pathway will be true for new teacher educators developing their skills in a new role.

This view of progression through three models of mentoring may not be entirely as intended by Furlong and Maynard but it does raise some important issues, particularly about the needs of trainees at different points in the training experience and about the way the professional relationship develops over time. It is some years since Maynard and Furlong (1995: 179) made a very significant observation when they wrote, 'It is because students typically go through different stages of learning to teach that we suggest that mentoring needs to be developmental too'. This is hugely important in developing a programme of school based training. Recognising this progression in training and adapting to it is a major challenge for any mentor. This point will be developed later.

So what are the priorities for mentors? The remainder of this chapter will be based on the three main themes that lie at the heart of mentoring of trainee teachers:

- how best to structure support for training;
- how to provide appropriate challenge;
- how to help trainees maximise the benefits of their training experience.

Support for training – planning and practice

The two most significant foundations on which to build school based training are the training framework and the classroom practice.

The overall framework for the training (usually in the form of a training plan) is best viewed as consisting of three levels. First is the overall training plan for the year which is individualised at the outset of the programme. This is the large-scale overview for the year. At the second level, this is divided into manageable chunks, usually based on school half terms and individualised to the needs of the trainee. The third level is the weekly meeting where the individualised training plan is turned into immediate action points. This means reviewing progress so far and identifying the next steps. These are the learning opportunities for the trainee and may well be expressed as targets. This aspect of your support as a mentor is covered later.

In school-based training the main focus is on the time trainees spend developing their practice in the classroom. This will begin by observing colleagues, particularly you as the mentor. The importance of this should not be overlooked but nor should the fact that new trainees often do not know what to look for in a lesson so need to have a reason to observe, not just an opportunity to do so. Geen and Harris (2002) were right to emphasise the importance of the mentor–trainee discussion in making sense of what they have seen, including the underlying purposes that support the viewed practice.

They expressed it like this:

> At the very outset collaborative teaching should enable students to observe their mentors modelling good practice. Subsequent dialogue should be a genuine learning experience for students. Hence, mentors should be prepared not just to offer advice and 'teaching tips' but to discuss their pedagogic skills analytically and to examine the deeper educational thinking which underpins the procedures they demonstrate. Geen and Harris (2002: 8)

From this starting point trainees can participate in elements of the lesson, such as working with small groups or taking key parts of the lesson. Moving from this to planning and teaching the whole lesson needs considered support. In the early stages the mentor can be most effective by being actively involved before, during and after each lesson. Support will have a number of elements:

Before the lesson:

- guidance with overall lesson planning including: curriculum content, learning intentions, teaching strategies, learning activities and assessment of/for learning.

During the lesson:

- complete a lesson observation against the lesson plan and in the context of relevant Teachers' Standards (DfE, 2012). (The written observation should normally use a proforma designed for ITT and familiar to the trainee.)

After the lesson:

- conversation to aid the trainee's own reflection on the lesson, structured feedback and shared identification of targets for improvement.

Together this approach will provide a good level of support and challenge within a structure that can be adapted as your trainee gains in both competence and confidence.

 Activity 7.2

Exploring aspects of mentor support

1. How will this three-part approach work in your school context?
2. How will the nature of support change with time?
3. How does this relate to Maynard and Furlong's three models?

Feedback must be aimed at helping the trainee to reflect on their own practice to help make sense of the complexity of working with pupils. Reflective practice in the context of initial teacher training is of fundamental importance for the professional development of the trainee. It is much more than keeping a record. It is through the thoughtful critique of their own experience that trainees make sense of the complex role of a teacher, develop their own pedagogical understanding and gradually become the kind of professional they want to be. It is also the case that critical reflection applies to the mentor and the trainee in the collaborative venture that is teacher training. This aspect of working together inevitably calls for a more equal and open relationship between the mentor and trainee. This is a gradual journey but you as a mentor need to know from the start that your role will evolve along with the changing needs of your trainee.

Appropriate challenge

The aspect of lesson feedback that school based trainers initially find most difficult is usually expressed as 'target setting'. Although most people acknowledge the importance of these 'small steps of improvement', 'stepping stones for development' or other appropriate metaphor, they can be hard to pin down. Apart from spotting what the real priorities are, which itself can be difficult, the main concerns are about making targets meaningful and ensuring nothing important gets missed. There is also the question of 'how many?'

How do you spot the priorities for targets?

New mentors can be very concerned about getting the right focus for targets following a lesson observation. If this concerns you then bear the following in mind. The lesson planning may itself suggest some areas to look for in a lesson observation. Trainees find it very helpful when there is prior agreement about the focus of the observation and this will automatically guide some of the post-lesson discussion and often lead to an appropriate theme for a target. Other areas will emerge during the lesson observation and in many cases trainees will identify these themselves, possibly with some prompting. It is more powerful to use themes suggested by trainees as targets because all those things about ownership will come into play. Whatever you do don't have too many targets. Three in one week will usually be enough but it is the next point that matters most.

How do you make targets meaningful?

Although the 'SMART' acronym (**S**pecific, **M**easurable, **A**chievable, **R**ealistic, and **T**ime-related) is widely used, and can be very helpful, it misses an important dimension that leaves it incomplete. It has far more value when extended to 'SMART<u>ER</u>' where the 'E' stands for 'evaluated' and the 'R' for 'Reviewed' (or 'revised,' 'refocused' or 'revisited' as necessary). This does more than complete the process but also builds in a degree of continuity in the targets. 'ER' also helps to focus on what has been done and this is the secret of meaningful targets. A target that is really no more than a title is not enough. A meaningful target will leave the trainee clear about the focus and the means of achieving it.

How do you ensure nothing important gets missed?

If all targets are drawn from the observation of lessons there is every possibility that they will not give a comprehensive training experience. Not everything that a teacher does will be directly observable in a lesson. This is one reason why the overall training plan is such an important framework for the training experience. The half-termly plan will break this down and give areas for action that provide further targets.

Target setting can therefore be viewed as coming from two directions. Some targets are **proactive** (set out in the advanced planning) and some **reactive** (drawn from classroom observations). This is a healthy and helpful mix which ensures both complete coverage of the Teachers' Standards and a clear response to emerging needs. If target setting is only drawn from classroom practice it will lack overall coherence. If it is only drawn from advanced planning it may lack immediate relevance. Target setting which includes proactive and reactive elements, is meaningful for trainees and is monitored in a reasonable timescale will give a positive sense of progress and achievement.

Maximising the benefits of training

A year of school-based training is an intensive experience and one where many trainees make rapid progress, often demonstrating a good level of effectiveness in all aspects of their work by the mid-point in the year. This is frequently acknowledged by their colleagues but the effect on future development can be mixed. This corresponds with Stage 4 in what Furlong and Maynard (1995) have described as five 'Stages of Learning' in student teachers' development:

Stage 1:   Early idealism
Stage 2:   Personal survival
Stage 3:   Dealing with difficulties
Stage 4:   Hitting *(or reaching)* a plateau
Stage 5:   Moving on

Where trainees hit the plateau their mentor may ease off in the belief that programme requirements are being met in a consistent and confident way. Our experience suggests this is quite a common position. The plateau is a high level but it doesn't go any further.

On the other hand many mentors see this stage as the ideal time to adapt their approach as teacher educators with a view to supporting a different level of challenge. Some express this in terms of 'moving from good to outstanding'. This sense of 'moving on' demands something different from the trainee and also from the teacher educator. By this point in the training year trainees have typically moved the focus of their thinking from their teaching to the learning of their pupils. With encouragement this will give a deeper engagement with conditions for learning and pedagogy in general. Trainees will seek to justify the choices they make and their reflective practice will have a more critical edge to it. This inevitably changes the nature of the dialogue with mentors and can be quite demanding not least because of the challenge to articulate what is 'known' as a teacher (see also Chapter 4).

For your reflection

There is no doubt that the role of teacher educator is a demanding one but it also brings professional rewards from a shared commitment to learning. By now you will be appreciating some of the ways in which the role of teacher educator will impact on your work as a teacher and your own professional development.

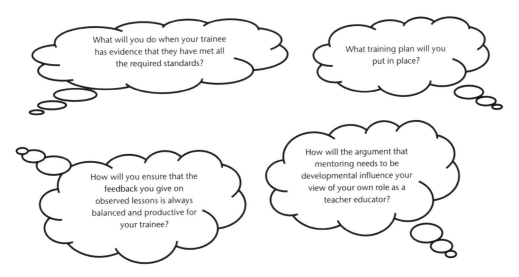

Figure 7.2   Reflecting on how to provide the right mix of support and challenge

 Further reading

- Punter, A. (2007) *Mentor Development for Teacher Training. A Scenario-based Approach.* Hatfield: University of Hertfordshire Press.
  This is a helpful book for teacher mentors to use individually or in groups, to consider different aspects of their role.

8

Practical and experiential support for trainees

Lynn Chapman and Bushra Connors

> This chapter covers two strategies for nurturing trainees as they face the demands of training to become a teacher:
>
> - Semi-structured interviews;
> - Forum Theatre and Augusto Boal.

Our approach to nurturing trainees through demanding experiences is based on finding ways to enable trainees to share the rich experiences of thinking and practice they gain while they are in school. The experiences of each trainee are unique, contextual and varied. The activities discussed in this chapter allow the collective experience of all the trainees and teacher educators to be brought to bear upon issues which trainees may be experiencing. We find that in using these activities we enhance our support for all trainees including those who are having difficulties. We use two main strategies: semi-structured interviews between trainees about their experiences in school, and drama in the form of Forum Theatre.

Semi-structured interviews

The objective of this strategy is that trainees use a provided set of semi-structured interview questions to gain an understanding of others' experience of schools, and therefore a wider perspective than that experienced in their own school. Trainees use a set of questions to interview another group/individual and then swap roles. Findings can be posted on an electronic forum or used as a basis for discussion.

Questions box: for trainees to use when interviewing each other

Theme 1 Teaching: How to make explanations/instructions/ expectations clear
1. Can you give me an example of how you have scaffolded a task to make it more accessible?
2. What ways have you found to communicate effectively?
3. What strategies do you use to overcome lack of understanding?

Theme 2 Developing your teacher presence
1. Can you tell us how you got yourself accepted as the class teacher?
2. What sorts of things did you do to manage nerves and create a positive presence?
3. What characteristics does a confident teacher exhibit?

Theme 3 Building relationships with learners
1. How do you plan to include all learners in your lessons?
2. How do you know when you can use humour to good effect in the classroom?
3. How do you earn trust in the classroom?

 Activity 8.1

Interviewing colleagues

- Use the questions in the questions box to interview some of your colleagues about their strategies in the areas listed.
- Make a note of any key points of interest that you might consider using in your own practice. What do they do differently from you?

 Activity 8.2

Group interviewing

This is best done after trainees have spent several weeks in school. Trainees are divided into groups of two to three people. Each group chooses a theme from the questions box and interviews the other groups about it. Some exemplar questions have been given. At the end each group presents a few key points that they have discovered as a result of this research.

We find that this activity has the effect of developing good relationships within the group as well as exposing trainees to the variety of practices that their peers will know about. It also introduces trainees to elementary research skills which some of them will find useful in developing enquiry-based research (see Chapter 10). A teacher educator using this strategy shares their response: 'It was really revealing and brought up some interesting points. For example one trainee thought that setting out all their expectations at the start would be a good idea. We reflected upon the most realistic and non-confrontational ways to set out expectations for a new class.'

Forum Theatre and Augusto Boal

In our work with trainees we also make productive use of drama. We found that through using particular forms of drama, trainees could bring their collective experience to bear on a problem which had been outlined in some detail by a trainee who was experiencing difficulties. The activities we designed are based on the work of Augusto Boal (Boal and Jackson, 1992; Boal, 1998). Boal, a Brazilian theatre director, developed a new type of theatre in the 1960s. Believing that theatre could be useful for people to learn new strategies to make changes to their world, Boal developed his Forum Theatre in order to help participants become more aware of aspects of problems they may not have previously considered. In Forum Theatre Boal undoes the traditional roles of actor and audience. The drama can focus on issues such as dealing with pupils with challenging behaviour or complex professional interactions in school. Through the use of scenarios representing the characters, actors and audience interact and discuss alternative outcomes. The trainee bringing the issue to the group outlines the scenario in some detail. The piece needs to be prepared and rehearsed by a small number of people and then performed in front of the rest of the group. Once the piece has been performed in its entirety, without interruption, it is performed again and this time any member of the audience can stop the action and take the place of an actor to try to bring about an alternative ending. To do this they say 'stop' and make their suggestion, such as the repositioning of an actor or object, the suggestion of a phrase or an action. The drama then continues until someone else wants to intervene or a changed outcome of the situation is reached. In this way participants are 'spectators' and work together to find solutions to the problem. The responses of some trainees involved in this activity are shared in Figure 8.1.

We used Forum Theatre in two ways: in the first instance the teacher and pupil roles are assigned, but the teacher is unaware of the roles assigned to the pupils to reflect a real classroom situation. The group then performs a classroom scene (e.g. starting a lesson) with each person acting according to their assigned role. This activity is then followed up with a discussion. In the second instance, trainees write, rehearse and act out their own piece from a recent experience that caused concern. This piece is then performed in front of the whole group and worked on collectively using the following rules.

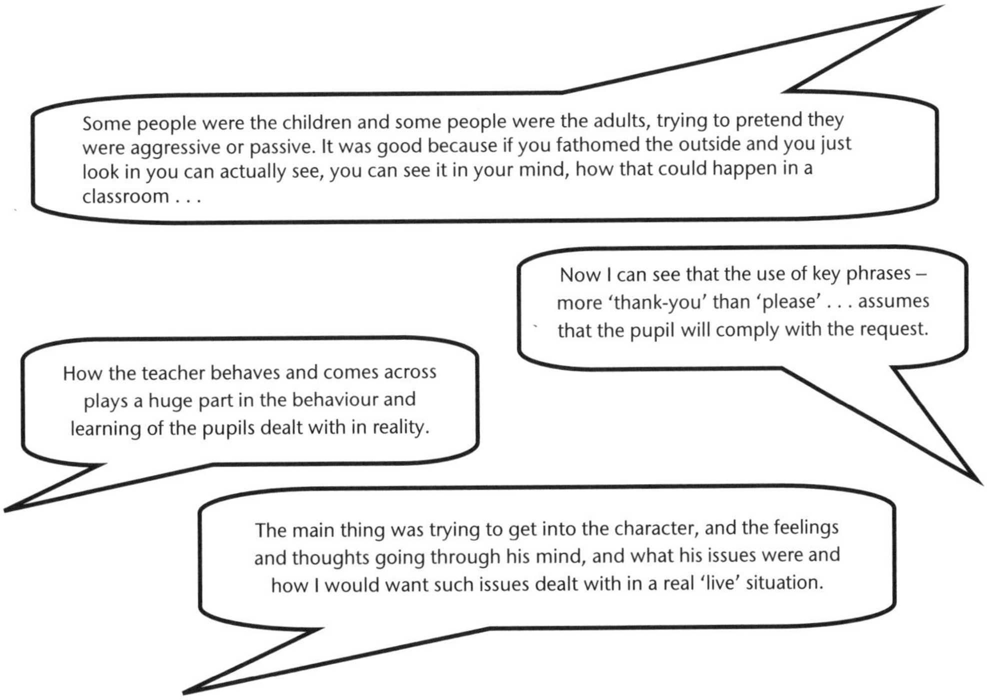

Some people were the children and some people were the adults, trying to pretend they were aggressive or passive. It was good because if you fathomed the outside and you just look in you can actually see, you can see it in your mind, how that could happen in a classroom . . .

Now I can see that the use of key phrases – more 'thank-you' than 'please' . . . assumes that the pupil will comply with the request.

How the teacher behaves and comes across plays a huge part in the behaviour and learning of the pupils dealt with in reality.

The main thing was trying to get into the character, and the feelings and thoughts going through his mind, and what his issues were and how I would want such issues dealt with in a real 'live' situation.

Figure 8.1   Responses to Forum Theatre

Rules box: Forum Theatre Rules as developed in our work with trainees

- Teacher and pupils need to be defined characters.
- Teacher's original solution must contain at least one error.
- The piece must be framed so as to discuss a concrete issue.

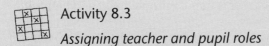

Activity 8.3

Assigning teacher and pupil roles

Assign trainees to the teacher and pupil roles (see pupil and teacher scenarios below).

While the 'pupils' read their roles and decide how they will behave for each of the three teacher types – you meet with the 'teacher(s)' and help them work out phrases they will use as they enact each teacher type.

To develop this, ask one group to act out their scenario for the whole group. The spectators (trainees) use the principle of Forum Theatre to stop the action and redirect it.

Pupil and Teacher scenarios:

Chris (pupil): You try to avoid doing any work because you find most of it boring and it has no significance to the things you are interested in. If you are challenged by the teacher you are quick to respond in a fairly abrupt manner. If the teacher is non-confrontational and helpful you respond in a positive way.

Sam (pupil): You try to avoid doing any work because you find reading and writing difficult. In particular you keep losing your place on the page or on the board so any work that entails copying is very difficult for you and you rarely complete these tasks, e.g. writing the learning objectives. If the teacher challenges you in a confrontational way you get embarrassed and just look down and start picking at your sleeve – you won't start working – and you only reply in grunts! If the teacher is non-confrontational and helpful you respond in a positive way.

Taz (pupil): You don't like the lesson to start as you don't want to do any writing so you try to keep the teacher busy by asking lots of questions. This doesn't necessarily have to be on the topic being taught! If the teacher tells you to be quiet then you still ask lots of questions because at least it looks like you're keen. If the teacher is non-confrontational and at least acknowledges there will be a time for questions later you respond in a positive way.

Charlie (pupil): You are a very keen pupil and want to do well but you are fed up with all the time-wasters in the class, so you start off by telling everyone else to shut up and sit down. When this doesn't work you get out your *National Geographic Book of Everything* to read. You're not disruptive and just quietly get on with your own thing ignoring the teacher. If the teacher is non-confrontational, makes the start of the lesson interesting and is helpful, however, you respond in a positive way.

Paulie (pupil): You are very disorganised and spend ages looking for your books and pencils at the start of the lesson. As you can never find them you go round asking everyone else for a pen and paper. You are fed up that teachers pick on you because at the start of every lesson they always shout at you – so you shout back. If the teacher is non-confrontational and helpful, however, you respond in a positive way.

The Teacher: You are just starting your second placement and are having difficulty getting the class settled at the start of the lesson. Things are not easy because the class have had a string of teachers before you and there is no set routine. You are anxious because you know you are being observed by your mentor so you must get the lesson off to a brisk start otherwise you won't get through everything. You are frustrated and this shows in the tone of your voice and your body language which only makes things worse. Act out this scene.

Activity 8.4

Using trainee generated scenarios

Choose a scenario from your experience to highlight a problem you have faced in your professional life. Recreate the situation in as much detail as possible and then act it out with a small group of trusted colleagues. You will need to agree that any discussion stays within the group and confidentiality is maintained.

Act out the piece again, but this time the spectators can stop the performance and make suggestions to change the outcome to a more positive one.

Discuss how the outcome might have been different if the actors had behaved differently.

How does this activity help you to view the situation from different perspectives?

We appreciate that many people are not comfortable with performing drama pieces or taking part in role-play activities, however, we urge you to try these techniques for three reasons. Firstly, drama can help bridge the theory–practice divide by giving trainees the opportunity to experience the skills of managing difficulties in action. Secondly, participants will be engaged on an emotional level and this is important if you are trying to bring about changes in behaviour. Thirdly, drama is more memorable than just talking or reading. In our experience, we found that one of the benefits of these drama activities was the creation of a safe environment to allow trainees to be honest and open about their concerns. It allows for scaffolding in strategies, by both peers and staff. It also creates a space in which the emotional aspects of becoming a teacher can be explored in a non-threatening and constructive way.

When things go wrong

In this chapter we have deliberately refrained from identifying the characteristics of a struggling trainee teacher as people change and develop at different rates and we believe starting with a deficit model can be counterproductive. If trainees are to take risks, there will be times when they do not achieve the targets they were setting out to reach. If the trainee is identified as struggling early, then there is more chance of working with them to overcome the problem. As a teacher mentor or tutor you need to be aware of the other professionals involved in the training, who will support both you and your trainee.

It is important to recognise that learning to teach involves emotions and that these play an essential role in developing as a teacher. The strategies outlined in this chapter allow you to bring these feelings out into the open and deal with them in a positive way. Using these strategies as a teacher educator and as a beginning teacher may feel 'clunky' at first, much like changing gear when learning to drive, but we hope this chapter and its associated activities will help you to realise that with time and practice an informed, critical and reflective teaching style can be achieved.

 For your reflection

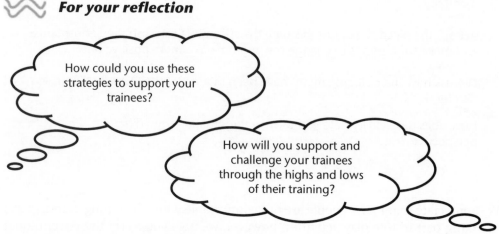

Figure 8.2 Reflecting on supporting trainees

Further reading

- **Behaviour Challenge** www.teachersmedia.co.uk/behaviourchallenge
  These video clips of classroom scenarios are interactive and allow choice of outcomes when dealing with classroom behaviour. They can stimulate useful discussion with your trainees.

- Campbell, A. and Kane, I. (1998) *School-based Teacher Education: Telling Tales from a Fictional Primary School.* London: David Fulton.
  This book includes narrative studies of struggling and successful trainees and their mentors.

- Zwozdiak-Myers, P. (2012) *The Teacher's Reflective Practice Handbook. Becoming an Extended Professional through Capturing Evidence-Informed Practice.* Abingdon: Routledge.
  This handbook is a useful source of guidance and ideas for trainees and practising teachers. It is underpinned by both theory and research and includes a range of reflective tasks, all helping towards building a trainee's portfolio of evidence.

9

Developing your practice through engaging with educational literature

Lara Fuller, Hilary Taylor and Amanda Roberts

This chapter covers a rationale for engaging with educational literature. It explores:

- the development of teacher professionalism;
- the interdependent nature of theory and practice;
- various purposes of engaging with the educational literature;
- how engagement with the literature can have an impact on professional practice.

This chapter explores a rationale for engaging with educational literature. It begins with some provocations around what it means to be a professional educator. It moves on to propose some key ways that engagement with theory can have an impact on the development of trainees' values and linked classroom practices. It ends with a discussion of ways in which both teacher educators and trainees might use such engagement with educational theory to support their CPD.

The development of teacher professionalism

We need to underpin any consideration of the development of practice by developing our understanding of what it means to be a professional teacher. In Chapter 3, we discussed ways in which teacher identity is developed. It may be useful here to think about the growth of teacher professionalism as part of that identity development. What, then, does it mean to be a professional?

The Teachers' Standards (DfE, 2011) offer one way of conceptualising teacher professionalism. Through proposing a number of professional attributes, knowledge and understanding and professional skills, the standards attempt to define the characteristics which teachers should exhibit at each stage of their career.

 Activity 9.1

Exploring teacher professionalism

Download the Teachers' Standards from:
https://www.education.gov.uk/publications/standard/publicationDetail/
Page1/DFE-00066-2011

Review the standards with the following questions in mind:

- What view of professionalism do the standards give?
- The standards describe the professional characteristics which teachers will be judged against when progressing through their career. What are the advantages and disadvantages, in your view, of this type of assessment system?

The Teachers' Standards offer one approach to defining professionalism. However, it is important that trainees explore, surface and articulate their own beliefs about what it means to be a professional teacher and that they use these beliefs to underpin their developing practice. We would suggest that our view of what it is to be a teacher is based on deep-seated values and beliefs. These may have had their inception in our own early experience of education or may have developed more recently. The following activity will help you to surface and reflect on the values and beliefs which drive your everyday practice. Other activities that can be used to explore your values can be found in Chapter 4.

 Activity 9.2

Exploring, surfacing and articulating your values

Use the questions in Figure 9.1 to explore, surface and articulate your own values and beliefs about your professional role as a teacher educator. What have been the key factors that have influenced your views and attitudes?

Use this same exercise with your trainees. How have your values and beliefs guided your practice?

What can you learn from this exercise about the development of the beliefs and values which guide your work?

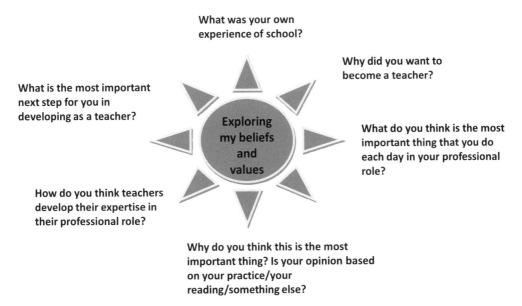

Figure 9.1   Exploring, surfacing and articulating your beliefs and values

Becoming the teacher you want to be

Ghaye and Ghaye (1998) suggest that, while values are fundamental to understanding ourselves as teachers and how we relate to others, they are likely to change in relation to context and circumstance. In order to maintain a sense of what you believe to be good practice – to become the teacher you want to be – you need to continually reflect on what it means to be a professional.

Hoyle (1975) offers an alternative way of viewing the development of professionalism. Using the word 'professionality' to describe the knowledge, skills and procedures used by teachers in their day-to-day teaching, he introduces the concept of restricted and extended professionality. Figure 9.2 illustrates the characteristics and behaviours of teachers at the extremes of the restricted-extended professionality continuum.

The notion of an extended professional is idealised. However, it provides a stimulus to support us in developing into more outward facing professionals. Bottery and Wright (2000: 484) suggest that 'education transcends the classroom', claiming that teachers need to understand their professional role in relation to the wider socio-political environment in which they work. It is within this broader context that teachers have to establish their own identity as professional educators. What then do trainees draw upon in order to support this development?

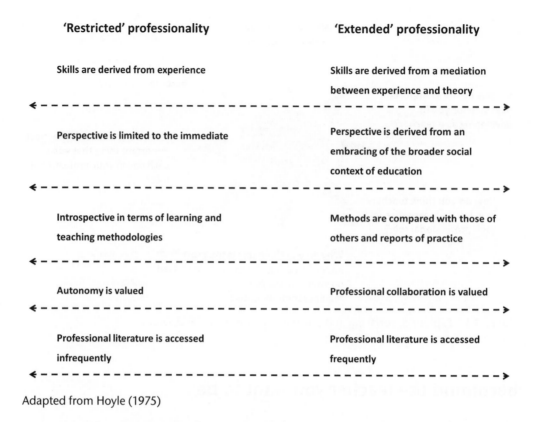

'Restricted' professionality	'Extended' professionality
Skills are derived from experience	Skills are derived from a mediation between experience and theory
Perspective is limited to the immediate	Perspective is derived from an embracing of the broader social context of education
Introspective in terms of learning and teaching methodologies	Methods are compared with those of others and reports of practice
Autonomy is valued	Professional collaboration is valued
Professional literature is accessed infrequently	Professional literature is accessed frequently

Adapted from Hoyle (1975)

Figure 9.2   Restricted and extended professionality

Activity 9.3

Exploring the concept of restricted and extended professionality

It might be interesting to think about your own place on the restricted–extended professionality continuum. Place an **X** on each dotted arrow in Figure 9.2 to show your current position. Join the **X**s together to make a line pattern. You might want to ask trainees to undertake the same activity and then consider together how you might interpret the different line patterns.

- What do you learn about yourself as a professional from this activity?
- Has this activity suggested any areas of professional development for you?

The interdependent nature of educational theory and practice

Trainee teachers naturally focus their attention on the day-to-day imperatives of classroom practice. In order to encourage them to consider the possible influences and reasons for what happens in their classroom, they need to move first to engage in 'reflection-on-action' and then to 'reflection-in-action' (Schön, 1983).

In the first activity, teachers think about their practice once it has taken place. Once they become more experienced, they can draw on their skills, knowledge and understanding to react to provocations and potential learning situations as they happen. Much of what practised teachers do is therefore tacit, instinctive and born of experience. If trainees are to learn from more experienced colleagues, it is crucial that teacher educators make explicit both the principles which underpin their developing practice and the various stimuli to that development (see Chapter 4). Educational theory provides one such stimulus. Trainee teachers cannot always readily connect educational theory, as detailed in the literature, with their experience in the classroom (Alexander, 2004). Supporting trainees in engaging with this literature at this formative stage of their professional development provides them with the opportunity to draw on the alternative perspectives of experienced practitioners outside of their school context. These practitioners add to the wisdom of colleagues and should perhaps be viewed simply as 'distant colleagues'. Such engagement with more experienced colleagues can support trainees in testing their ideas, in critiquing what is happening in practice and in finding ways to develop into the teacher they wish to become.

Engaging with 'what is known' to support professional development

Professional knowledge can be captured and shared in numerous ways. Conversations with colleagues, watching Teachers' Media, reading an article in the professional press and so on can all provoke the thinking which leads to professional development. Accessing the literature is sometimes more problematic than the less formal learning opportunities offered by conversations, for example. However, determining the right type of literature to read to address your particular need is the first step in engaging positively with the accumulated wisdom of others, which can be accessed through the written word.

 Activity 9.4

Exploring the scope and purposes of engaging with educational literature

Educational texts can serve a number of purposes. Begin to explore this concept by linking the text to the purpose in Figure 9.3.

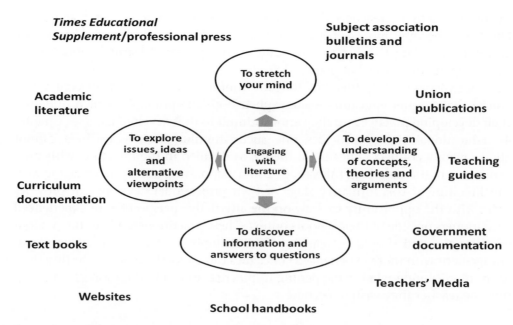

Figure 9.3   Exploring the scope and purposes of engaging with educational literature

Reading for a purpose

Identifying the purpose of your reading will help you to spend your time effectively. You may wish to read for some of the following reasons.

Extending your understanding of practice

An empowering outcome of reading can be that you become aware of the strengths of your practice, as you recognise that many of the effective aspects of teaching discussed within books and journals are things that you already do. We raised above the issue of the tacit nature of much teacher knowledge. Reading can help us to make explicit what is implicit about teaching (Baumfield and Butterworth, 2005) and thus support trainees' development. The process of sharing such tacit knowledge is both cognitive and social in nature (Lave and Wenger, 1991). Through discussing educational articles, you can help trainees to assign meaning to what they are reading, making links to existing knowledge structures and developing their classroom practice (see Figure 9.4a).

Developing your professional viewpoint

Whatever your purpose you need to read critically – that is, you need to question what is read, think about the assumptions on which it is based and the application of what has been learned to your own setting. Only then can you locate yourself in terms of the reading, that is, decide where you stand, what your view of the topic in question is and thus develop your own professional viewpoint. Having established your own position you can now also be aware of alternative perspectives and how they challenge your view. This can lead to interesting professional dialogue and a greater awareness of how you can respond to initiatives and challenges while maintaining you own values and principles (see Figure 9.4b).

Developing your professional voice

The development of your professional viewpoint allows you to develop a professional voice, to speak with confidence and authority about issues which concern you and which you may wish to change (see Figure 9.4c).

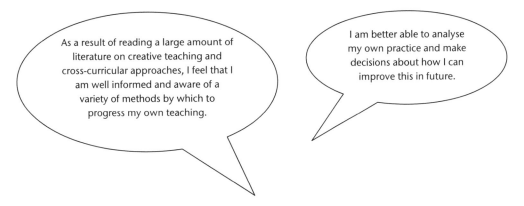

Figure 9.4a   Trainees extending their understanding of practice

Figure 9.4b   Trainees developing a professional viewpoint

Figure 9.4c   Trainees developing a professional voice

It is sometimes difficult to penetrate a complex piece of writing or to link what you are reading to what you already experience in your daily practice. The CONNECT – EXTEND – CHALLENGE thinking routine may help you to connect theory to your own developing practice.

Activity 9.5

Connecting theory to practice

Choose an article on a topic which is of interest to you. Use the following thinking prompts to help you to link what you are reading to your own developing practice:

CONNECT: How is what you are reading connected to what you already know?

EXTEND: How does what you are reading help you to extend your thinking?

CHALLENGE: What is challenging to you about what you are reading? What questions would you like to ask the author about what is written?

For further details of this approach see Visible Thinking in Action, a useful website for developing different ways of thinking, available at:

http://pzweb.harvard.edu/vt/VisibleThinking_html_files/01_ VisibleThinkingInAction/01a_VTInAction.html. In particular, the connect, extend, challenge prompts are found at http://pzweb.harvard.edu/vt/ VisibleThinking_html_files/03_ThinkingRoutines/03d_UnderstandingRoutines/ ConnectExtendChallenge/ConnectExtend_Routine.html.

In this chapter we have explored how an exploration of the educational literature might support teacher educators and trainee teachers in continuing to develop their professional practice. In Chapter 10 we move on to consider how teacher educators and trainees might begin adding to this body of written knowledge, through exploring your own practice and then sharing what you have learned with others within the profession.

For your reflection

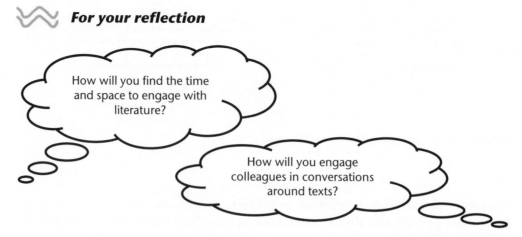

Figure 9.5   Reflecting on using literature

Further reading

- RSA Animate www.thersa.org/events/video/animate/rsa-animate-changing-paradigms.
  This website contains a number of animations which are a good stimulus for professional dialogue between teachers at any stage in their careers.
- Leach, J. and Moon, B. (2008) *The Power of Pedagogy.* London: Sage.
  This text explores key concepts in learning and teaching and draws on a wide range of traditions and examples of practice. It is a text from which you can draw examples for reflection and professional development and it can also be used to model engagement with reading in the field.

10

Practice-based enquiry as a basis for change

Amanda Roberts and Hilary Taylor

> This chapter covers a rationale for why teachers enquire into their own practice. It explores:
>
> - the impetus for practice-based enquiry;
> - a way of visualising the enquiry process which can be used to support coherent and effective action;
> - how to plan for, support and evaluate the impact of enquiry activity.

In Chapter 9 we discussed how an exploration of the educational literature might support teacher educators and trainee teachers in continuing to develop their professionalism. In this chapter we consider the impetus for practice-based enquiry where the desired result is a change. This change might be in individual, group or whole school practice, both within and beyond the organisation. We discuss the capacity of teacher educators and trainees to undertake such enquiry in order to develop their understanding of their own practice and to lead change. We consider how teachers might share what they have learned from such enquiry with professional peers, with the purpose of both informing practice more widely and increasing the capacity for change. Practice-based enquiry can be of benefit to all teachers, irrespective of their experience. This chapter is therefore directed at encouraging both teacher educators and trainees, under the generic term of 'teacher', to develop their practice through exploration and enquiry.

The impetus and capacity to effect change through practice-based enquiry

Why should teachers want to bring about change in their classroom and beyond? Schools are complex organisations and it is natural that many teachers may not see it as their place to begin to alter things. It might seem logical to argue that such activity should be reserved for the leadership team and those in positions of authority. Some writers however propose an alternative view. Lawrence Stenhouse for example, writing in 1975, suggested that curriculum development rests on the study of classrooms. Introducing here the idea of enquiry as a vehicle of classroom and wider change, he argued, moreover, that 'it is not enough that teachers' work should be studied: they need to study it for themselves' (1975: 143). Similarly, Durrant and Holden (2006) claim that teachers are in the position to best understand the complexities of school life and professional practice, and that they should apply this knowledge to improve not only their own practice but to influence school improvement. Furthermore, they suggest that direct involvement in enquiry and school improvement should be the main focus of teachers' professional activity and learning. Our understanding of this important concept of autonomy can be developed by a consideration of Bandura's (1989) concept of 'agency'. Bandura saw human beings as able to affect changes in themselves and their situation through the exercise of their own efforts. This human agency is based on a sense of self, resting on an individual's values and beliefs and leading to an ability to pursue goals through strategic action (Frost, 2006). Such action is construed by Frost as leadership, where leading development and innovation is not the province of only those with leadership position but of all who have an appetite for change. In this view of the world of the school, all teachers are seen as having an implicit potential to exercise leadership (Frost, 2011).

Visualising an enquiry process – the enquiry tree

Many teachers may be used to the process of research; however, they may be less well attuned to enquiry. So what is the difference? A wide range of activities can be identified under the definition of 'practitioner enquiry', such as action research, reading to inform practice and reflection (Wilkins, 2012). In this chapter, we use the word 'enquiry' to signify a process of investigation where the desired result is a change: a change in understanding, a change in perception, a change in practice. This change is envisaged as being led by the teacher, in a process that does not rely on hierarchy but which draws on the individual's innate capacity for leadership (Frost, 2006).

The cycle of action research suggested by McNiff (2010) provides another way of conceptualising the enquiry process. Here, teachers begin by identifying an area of focus which is of interest to them, arising out of their values and beliefs, and to which they wish to make a difference. They then clarify the purpose of their enquiry. For example, they may wish to understand an element of their practice in more depth, to change what they do in the classroom and evaluate it, or to pose a question about current school policy. They may decide to collaborate with colleagues to achieve their desired impact. Based on this purpose or desired impact, they adopt an enquiry approach which will allow them to investigate their area of focus effectively and with appropriate rigour. They devise a plan of action and carry out some activity, collecting data as they go. This activity and data may take a number of different forms. Teachers may, for example:

- do something differently in the classroom and then collect data to illuminate its impact;

- interview some students and then put their suggestions into action, interviewing them again to see the impact of this change;

- work with a colleague to observe one another's lessons, meeting at lunchtime to engage in a professional dialogue about what they have seen and learned;

- set up a working group to share teaching ideas, try them out and discuss how effective they have been in meeting their aims.

Once they have taken some action, they move on to organise, analyse and interpret their data, looking for patterns and themes which help them to understand more about their area of focus. Finally, they evaluate the impact of their enquiry activity, deciding on what has changed through it and on the new questions which arise. They plan how they can share their new knowledge with others.

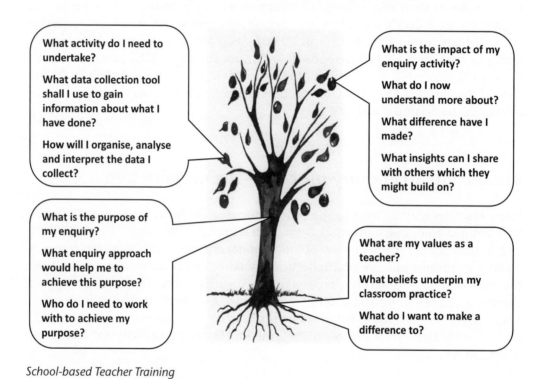

School-based Teacher Training
© Elizabeth White and Joy Jarvis 2013

Figure 10.1   The enquiry tree

This sequence of events is encapsulated in the image of *the enquiry tree*, shown in Figure 10.1. (This image is photocopiable for use in your school or institution.) The image of the tree is significant in a number of ways. It suggests that:

- enquiry needs to be rooted in a teacher's values and beliefs if it is to have any real impact;

- the purpose of an individual enquiry needs to arise from these beliefs and values and be translated into an appropriate enquiry approach;

- the enquiry approach provides a firm structure and details the appropriate methods by which the stated purpose is to be achieved;
- key findings, both intentional and unexpected, will branch from the enquiry process;
- the fruit of the enquiry needs to be noted, articulated and shared.

Finally, the whole enquiry process needs to be organic, to be open to changes and to have an internal coherence which arises from each stage building on the previous one and being part of a single, growing structure.

Planning and undertaking your enquiry

The following activities arise from *the enquiry tree* and could be undertaken to help you to plan and undertake the first three stages of the enquiry process. Two examples of how teachers have translated this guidance into action are given for each activity (see Figure 10.2).

 Activity 10.1

Stage 1: Exploring my values, beliefs and my area of focus

Before you begin your enquiry you need to understand what is driving you to focus on your particular area of interest. Jot down some notes to answer each of the questions below.

- What are my values as a teacher?
- What beliefs underpin my classroom practice?
- What do I want to make a difference to?

See Figure 10.2a for teachers' comments on exploring their values.

 Activity 10.2

Stage 2: Determining purpose and approach

You now need to determine the purpose of your enquiry and therefore what the most appropriate approach might be. Jot down some notes to answer each of the questions below.

- What is the purpose of my enquiry?
- What enquiry approach would help me to achieve this purpose?
- Who do I need to work with to achieve my purpose?

See Figure 10.2b for teachers' comments about their approach.

I am concerned about the way in which my students seem to be disengaged from the learning process. They seem to leave me to do all the work. I believe that we learn best if we take an active role. I want to find ways to help my students become more active learners.

I believe that all children should be given the opportunity to access the curriculum fully. I believe that reading is the key to this. If students can't read they are at a disadvantage. I struggled with reading myself when I first started school and suppose this is why this is dear to my heart. I want to make a difference to the way in which we support children who have difficulty developing their reading.

Figure 10.2a Comments of teachers using the guidance: exploring their values:

I want to develop new ways of involving students in lessons. I want to make sure that they understand the way in which learning takes place and then give them the opportunity to actually lead some parts of lessons themselves.

I want to develop some new ways of supporting the development of reading in my classroom and maybe beyond that. Some of the children don't like to admit that they struggle with reading. I want to create a culture in which it is OK to admit you need help. I also want to try out some new strategies to support children in developing their reading in a fun way. I'm going to start by seeing if any of the other teachers want to work with me on this.

Figure 10.2b Comments of teachers using the guidance: determining their purpose and approach

Developing active learners is a focus for my department so we are all going to trial different ways of doing this and then compare what we learned. I'm going to work with four students to prepare them to lead starter activities in two lessons. A colleague will observe the starters and then we will discuss how it went. I will also ask all the class to fill in a smiley-face sheet to show their views and talk with the students leading the starters to gain their views.

My colleague and I are going to work together to develop and trial some new reading strategies to see what works. We want to develop some fun ideas which children really want to have a go at and see if that helps them to develop a more positive attitude to their reading. We are going to try this for a couple of weeks and then chat with the children to see what impact it is having on their confidence and attitude towards reading.

Figure 10.2c Comments of teachers using the guidance: taking action

Activity 10.3

Stage 3: Doing something and collecting and interpreting information about what I have done

You now need to plan and undertake some activity and then collect some data which will help you to understand its impact. Jot down some notes to answer each of the questions below.

- What activity do I need to undertake?
- What data collection tool shall I use to gain information about what I have done?
- How will I organise, analyse and interpret the data I collect?

See Figure 10.2c for teachers' comments on action taken.

Planning for and evaluating impact

It is important that teachers plan for the impact they wish to achieve through their enquiry activity. This planning process makes it far more likely that their enquiry will lead to the desired outcomes. In Figure 10.3, impact is imagined as the fruits of the enquiry tree, the end product of your activity. Like fruit, impact is often slow growing and can be seen to be developing throughout the enquiry process, rather than simply being a discrete product achieved at the end. Figure 10.3 indicates the types of outcome you might hope for from your enquiry.

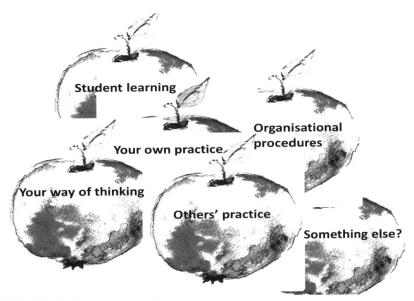

Figure 10.3 The fruits of your enquiry

Activity 10.4

Planning for and evaluating impact

You might want to consider these questions at an early stage in your enquiry planning.

- What impact do you hope to achieve from your enquiry?
- How will you know that you have been successful in achieving this impact?

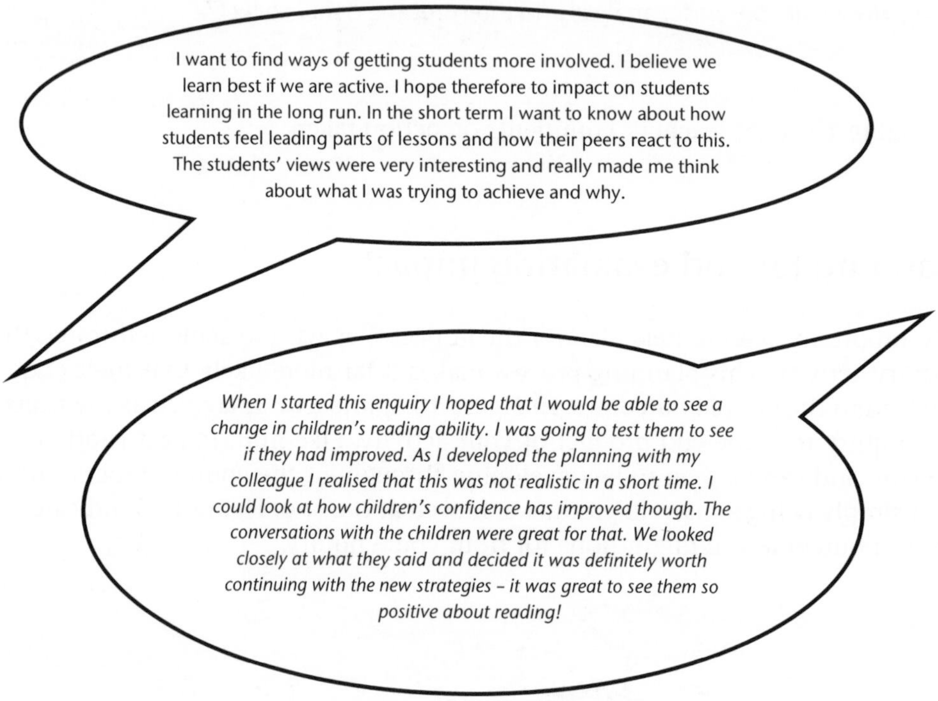
I want to find ways of getting students more involved. I believe we learn best if we are active. I hope therefore to impact on students learning in the long run. In the short term I want to know about how students feel leading parts of lessons and how their peers react to this. The students' views were very interesting and really made me think about what I was trying to achieve and why.
When I started this enquiry I hoped that I would be able to see a change in children's reading ability. I was going to test them to see if they had improved. As I developed the planning with my colleague I realised that this was not realistic in a short time. I could look at how children's confidence has improved though. The conversations with the children were great for that. We looked closely at what they said and decided it was definitely worth continuing with the new strategies – it was great to see them so positive about reading!

Figure 10.4a Teachers considering the impact of their enquiry

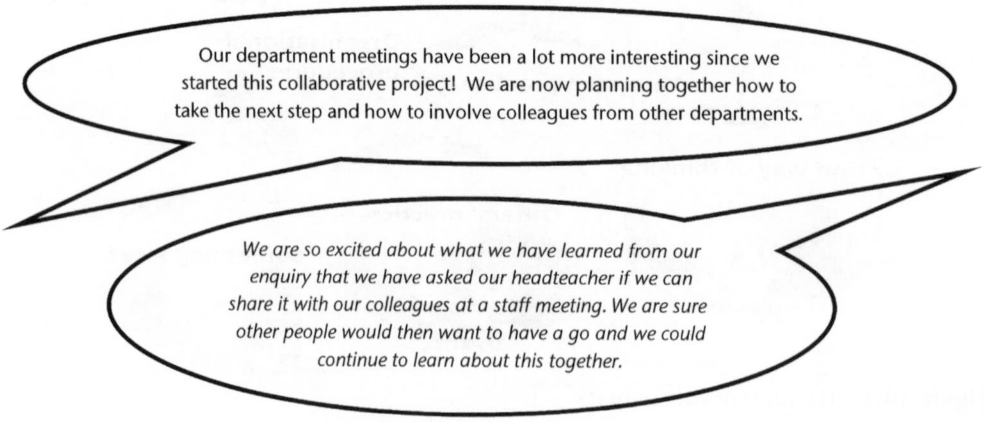
Our department meetings have been a lot more interesting since we started this collaborative project! We are now planning together how to take the next step and how to involve colleagues from other departments.
We are so excited about what we have learned from our enquiry that we have asked our headteacher if we can share it with our colleagues at a staff meeting. We are sure other people would then want to have a go and we could continue to learn about this together.

Figure 10.4b Teachers sharing their enquiries

Sharing what you have learned

It is important that teachers share the learning which arises from an enquiry process. This allows what has been learned to have a wider impact and offers the potential for others to build on what is now known and understood or to develop their practice accordingly (see Figure 10.4a). It also increases the capacity for change. Knowledge can be shared in a number of ways, through informal discussions with colleagues, through the production of a poster or video, through presentations at meetings, through the writing of an article for a professional or academic journal and so on (see Figure 10.4b). You might find it useful to use the questions which inform each stage of the enquiry process as a template for writing a report of what you have discovered.

In this chapter the enquiry process has been conceptualised not only as a process of building knowledge but as a strategy to support change. We hope that you will enjoy and benefit from developing your skills, knowledge and understanding of how you can use practice based enquiry to lead change in your classroom school and beyond.

For your reflection

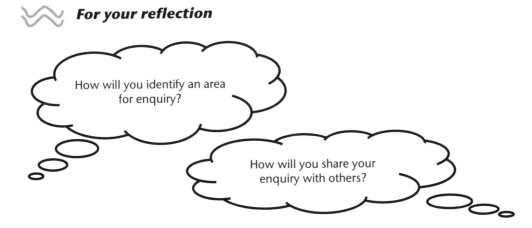

How will you identify an area for enquiry?

How will you share your enquiry with others?

Figure 10.5 Reflecting on your research opportunities

 ### *Further reading*

- Durrant, J. and Holden, G. (2006) *Teachers Leading Change: Doing Research for School Improvement.* London: Paul Chapman Publishing.
  This text explores ways in which teachers can use research to bring about school improvement.

- Koshy, V. (2010) *Action Research for Improving Educational Practice.* London: Sage. This text takes the reader through an action research process, identifying underlying principles and practical considerations. It contains a wide range of data collection approaches and gives useful examples that can be adapted as necessary.

- McNiff, J. (2010) *Action Research for Professional Development.* Dorset: September Books.

  This is a very useful book for first time action researchers who are looking to explore aspects of their practice.

References

Alexander, R. (2004) 'Still no pedagogy? principle, pragmatism and compliance in primary education', *Cambridge Journal of Education*, 34 (1): 7–33.

Bandura, A. (1989) 'Human agency in social cognitive theory', *American Psychologist*, 49 (9): 1175–84.

Baumfield, V. M. and Butterworth, A. M. (2005) *Systematic Review of the Evidence for the Impact of Teaching Thinking Skills on Teachers.* London: EPPI-Centre, Social Science Research Unit, Institute of Education.

Berry, A. and Loughran, J. (2002) 'Developing an understanding of learning to teach in teacher education', in J. Loughran and T. Russell (eds) *Improving Teacher Education Practices through Self-study.* London: RoutledgeFalmer.

Boal, A. (1998) *Theatre of the Oppressed.* London: Pluto.

Boal, A. and Jackson, A. (1992) *Games for Actors and Non-actors.* London: Routledge.

Bolam, R. (1993) 'Recent developments and emerging issues', in M. Williams and R. Bolam (eds) *The Continuing Professional Development of Teachers. Papers Presented for GTC.* London: Department for Education and Skills.

Bottery, M. and Wright, N. (2000) 'The directed profession: teachers and the state in the third millennium', *Journal of In-Service Education*, 26 (3): 475–87.

Boyd, P. and Harris, K. (2010) 'Becoming a university lecturer in teacher education: Expert school teachers reconstructing their pedagogy and identity', *Professional Development in Education*, 36 (1–2): 9–24.

Brookfield, S. (1995) *Becoming a Critically Reflective Teacher.* San Francisco: Jossey-Bass.

Campbell, A. and Kane, I. (1998) *School Based Teacher Education: Telling Tales from a Fictional Primary School.* London: David Fulton.

Chivers, L., Collins, C., Lee, L., Solly, D., Dickerson, C., Jarvis, J. and Levy, R. (2010) 'Enhancing the induction process of new teacher educators through a self-study group'. *International Conference on Self-Study of Teacher Education Practices*, Herstmonceux Castle.

Clemans, A., Berry, A. and Loughran, J. (2010) 'Lost and found in transition: The professional journey of teacher educators', *Professional Development in Education*, 36 (1–2): 211–28.

Cochran-Smith, M. (2003) 'Learning and unlearning: The education of teacher educators', *Teaching and Teacher Education*, 19: 5–28.

DFE (2011) *Teachers' Standards.* Available at www.education.gov.uk/publications (accessed 25 April 2012).

DFE (2012) *Teacher Appraisal and Capability.* Available at www.education.gov.uk/publications (accessed 25 April 2012).

Durrant, J. and Holden, G. (2006) *Teachers Leading Change: Doing Research for School Improvement.* London: Paul Chapman Publishing.

Francis, D. (1997) 'Critical incident analysis: A strategy for developing reflective practice', *Teachers and Teaching*, 3(2): 169–88.

Freedman, S., Lipson, B. and Hargreaves, D. (2008) *More Good Teachers.* Available at www.policyexchange.org.uk/publications (accessed 25 April 2012).

Frost, D. (2006) 'The concept of "agency" in leadership for learning', *Leading and Managing*, 12 (2): 19–28.

Frost, D. (2011) 'Supporting teacher leadership in 15 countries. International Teacher Leadership project. Phase 1. A report.' Available at http://www.leadershipforlearning.org.uk/images/LFL/itl_report_%2021_12_11.pdf (accessed 13 March 2012).

Furlong, J. and Maynard, T. (1995) *Mentoring Student Teachers: The growth of professional knowledge*. London: Routledge.

Geen, A. and Harris, C. (2002) 'Student perceptions of collaborative teaching in Initial Teacher Education and Training', *UWIC Education Papers*, 1: 1–11.

Ghaye, A. and Ghaye, K. (1998) *Teaching and Learning through Reflective Practice*. London: David Fulton.

Graham, S., Lester, N. and Dickerson, C. (in preparation) Discover-Deepen-Do: a 3D pedagogical approach for developing newly qualified teachers as professional learners.

Griffiths, V., Thompson, S. and Hryniewicz, L. (2010) 'Developing a research profile: mentoring and support for teacher educators', *Professional Development in Education*, 36 (1–2): 245–62.

Guskey, T. (2005) *Evaluating Professional Development: An interview with Dr. Thomas Guskey.* February 16, 2005. National College.

Haddon, M. (2003) *The Curious Incident of the Dog in the Night-Time.* London: Random House.

Haggarty, L. and Postlethwaite, K. (2012) 'An exploration of changes in thinking in the transition from student teacher to newly qualified teacher', *Research Papers in Education*, 27 (2): 241–62.

Hargreaves, A. (2007) 'Sustainable professional learning communities', in L. Stoll and K. S. Louis, (eds) *Professional Learning Communities*. Maidenhead: Open University Press.

Harrison, J. and McKeon, F. (2008) The formal and situated learning of beginning teacher educators in England: Identifying characteristics for successful induction in the transition from workplace in schools to workplace in higher education', *European Journal of Teacher Education*, 31: 151–68.

Hart, S., Dixon, A., Drummond, J. And McIntyre, D. (2004) *Learning Without Limits.* Maidenhead: Open University Press.

Hoyle, E. (1975) 'Professionality, professionalism and control in teaching', in V. Houghton et al. *Management in Education: The Management of Organisations and Individuals.* London: Ward Lock Educational in association with Open University Press.

Jarvis, J. and Iantaffi, A. (2006) '"Deaf people don't dance": challenging student teachers' perspectives of pupils and inclusion', *Deafness and Education International*, 8 (2): 75–87.

Jarvis, J. and Trodd, L. (2008) 'Other ways of seeing, other ways of being: Imagination as a tool for developing multiprofessional practice for children with communication needs', *Child Language, Teaching and Therapy*, 24: 211–27.

Lave, J. and Wenger, E. (1991) *Situated Learning: Legitimate Peripheral Participation.* Cambridge: Cambridge University Press.

Leach, J. and Moon, B. (2008) *The Power of Pedagogy*. London: Sage.

Lunenberg, M., Korthagen, F. and Swennen, A. (2007) 'The teacher educator as a role model', *Teaching and Teacher Education*, 23: 586–601.

Maynard, T. and Furlong, J. (1993) 'Learning to teach and models of mentoring', in D. McIntyre, H. Hagger and M. Wilkin (eds) *Mentoring: Perspectives on School-Based Teacher Education.* London: Kogan Page.

Maynard, T. and Furlong, J. (1995) 'Learning to teach and models of mentoring', in T. Kerry, and A. Mayes (eds) *Issues in Mentoring*. London: Routledge.

McKeon, F. and Harrison, J. (2010) 'Developing pedagogical practice and professional identities of beginning teacher educators', *Professional Development in Education*, 36 (1–2): 25–44.

McNiff, J. (2010) *Action Research for Professional Development*. Dorset: September Books.

Mezirow, J. (1990) *Fostering Critical Reflection in Adulthood: A Guide to Transformative and Emancipatory Learning*. London: Jossey-Bass.

Murray, J. and Male, T. (2005) 'Becoming a teacher educator: Evidence from the field', *Teaching and Teacher Education*, 21: 125–42.

O'Donoghue, T. and Clarke, S. (2010) *Leading Learning*. Abingdon: Routledge.

Russell, T. (2007) 'How experience changed my values as a teacher educator', in T. Russell, and J. Loughran (eds) *Enacting a Pedagogy of Teacher Education: Values, Relationships and Practices*. Abingdon: Routledge.

Schön, D. A. (1983) *The Reflective Practitioner: How Professionals Think in Action*. London: Arena Ashgate.

Shulman, L. S. (1987) 'Knowledge and teaching: Foundations of the new reform', *Harvard Educational Review*, 57: 1–22.

Stenhouse, L. (1975) *An introduction to Curriculum Research and Development*. London: Heinemann.

Stoll, L., Bolam, R., McMahon, A., Wallace, M. and Thomas, S. (2006) 'Professional learning communities: A review of the literature. *Journal of Educational Change*, 7: 221–58.

Swennen, A., Volman, M. and Van Essen, M. (2008) 'The development of the professional identity of two teacher educators in the context of Dutch teacher education', *European Journal of Teacher Education*, 31: 169–84.

TDA (2007) Developing trainees' subject knowledge for teaching. London. Available at http://dera.ioe.ac.uk/9688/ (accessed 25 April 2012).

Usher, R., Bryant, I. and Johnston, R. (1997) *Adult Education and the Postmodern Challenge: Learning Beyond the Limits*. London: Routledge.

Wenger, E. (1998) *Communities of Practice: Learning, Meaning and Identity*. Cambridge: Cambridge University Press.

White, E. (2011) 'Working towards explicit modelling: Experiences of a new teacher educator', *Professional Development in Education*, 37: 483–97.

White, E. (in preparation) Exploring the professional development needs of new teacher educators situated solely in school: Developing subject knowledge with student teachers.

Whitehead, J. and Fitzgerald, B. (2004) 'Experiencing and evidencing learning: New ways of working with mentors and trainees in a training school partnership', presentation to the AERA 04 Symposium: The transformative potential of individuals' collaborative self-studies for sustainable global educational networks of communication, in San Diego, 16 April, 2004.

Wilkins, R. (2012) *Research Engagement for School Development*. London: Institute of Education.

Young, J. and Erickson, L. (2011) 'Imagining, becoming and being a teacher: How professional history mediates teacher educator identity', *Studying Teacher Education*, 7 (2): 121–9.

Index